Activism in Architectu

This edited collection gathers contributions from a diverse range of renowned scholars and professionals to uncover the unique relationship between passive architectural systems and activism. Focusing on the pioneering work of the influential American chemist and inventor, Harold R. Hay (1909–2009), and the environmental awareness events that took hold in the United States during the 1960s and 1970s, the book assembles essays which closely examine Hay's contribution to architecture and the work of those who directly and tangentially were affected by it. The book also offers insights into the role of passive energy design today. Appealing to researchers, architects and students interested in architecture and design technology, *Activism in Architecture* explores the role of passive environmental inventions as an active agent in shaping socio-political debates.

Margot McDonald is Department Head and Professor of Architecture at California Polytechnic State University (Cal Poly), USA. She teaches an interdisciplinary design studio between architecture, construction, engineering, landscape and building design with an emphasis on building energy and environmental performance.

Carolina Dayer is an Architect and Assistant Professor in Architecture at the Aarhus School of Architecture, Denmark. In 2011 she founded her own architectural practice, Bottega 11, and she is one of the editors and author of *Confabulations: Storytelling in Architecture* (Routledge, 2016).

Routledge Research in Architecture

The *Routledge Research in Architecture* series provides the reader with the latest scholarship in the field of architecture. The series publishes research from across the globe and covers areas as diverse as architectural history and theory, technology, digital architecture, structures, materials, details, design, monographs of architects, interior design and much more. By making these studies available to the worldwide academic community, the series aims to promote quality architectural research.

For a full list of titles, please visit: www.routledge.com/Routledge-Research-in-Architecture/book-series/RRARCH.

Tradition as Mediation: Louis I. Kahn
The Dominican Motherhouse & The Hurva Synagogue
Dana Margalith

A History of Design Institutes in China
From Mao to Market
Charlie Xue and Guanghui Ding

A History of Russian Exposition and Festival Architecture
1700–2014
Edited by Alla Aronova and Alexander Ortenberg

Architectures of Transversality
Paul Klee, Louis Kahn and the Persian Imagination
Shima Mohajeri

Rome and the Legacy of Louis I. Kahn
Edited by Elisabetta Barizza and Marco Falsetti

Activism in Architecture
Bright Dreams of Passive Energy Design
Edited by Margot McDonald and Carolina Dayer

Activism in Architecture
Bright Dreams of Passive Energy Design

Edited by Margot McDonald
and Carolina Dayer

Routledge
Taylor & Francis Group

LONDON AND NEW YORK

First published 2019
by Routledge

2 Park Square, Milton Park, Abingdon, Oxfordshire OX14 4RN
52 Vanderbilt Avenue, New York, NY 10017

Routledge is an imprint of the Taylor & Francis Group, an informa business

First issued in paperback 2020

British Library Cataloguing-in-Publication Data
A catalogue record for this book is available from the British Library

Library of Congress Cataloging-in-Publication Data
Names: McDonald, Margot, editor. | Dayer, Carolina, editor.
Title: Activism in architecture : bright dreams of passive energy design /
edited by Margot McDonald and Carolina Dayer
Description: New York : Routledge, 2019. |
Series: Routledge research in architecture |
Includes bibliographical references and index.
Identifiers: LCCN 2018016547 | ISBN 9781138741430 (hardback) |
ISBN 9781315182858 (ebook)
Subjects: LCSH: Architecture and society–United States. |
Architecture and energy conservation–United States. |
Solar energy–Passive systems–United States. |
Environmentalism–United States. | Hay, H. R. (Harold R.)–Influence.
Classification: LCC NA2543.S6 A32 2019 | DDC 720.1/03–dc23
LC record available at https://lccn.loc.gov/2018016547

ISBN: 978-1-138-74143-0 (hbk)
ISBN: 978-0-367-66567-8 (pbk)

Typeset in Sabon
by Out of House Publishing

To Harold R. Hay

"This book is a testament to the grassroots pioneers of passive solar design and technology, and a catalog of both the potential of passive systems and the obstacles their champions have faced. Harold Hay was a visionary with his eye not on simple technological advancement, but on deep and wide-spread change to ways of building and consuming. This collection of rich and varied perspectives illuminates Hay's ideas through concrete examples and personal witness."

Edward Mazria, Architecture 2030, USA

"Harold Hay was a modernist who sought to resurrect some fundamental truths known to the ancient Chinese, Greeks, and Anasazis. This book revives his legacy and the dreams and actions of passive energy design activists that through architecture promote health, productivity, and delight for people."

Denis Hayes, President, Bullitt Foundation, USA

"*Activism in Architecture* assembles a robust history of the power that passive architectural systems, design integration, environmentalism, and technology have had on low-energy building design. Fifteen essays from influential educators, scientists, practitioners, and solar designers, exemplify the legacy and lessons of passive pioneer and solar inventor, Harold Hay. The book is a must-read for students of architecture, passive enthusiasts and activists, and future stewards of the environment."

Alison Kwok, University of Oregon, USA and Walter Grondzik, Ball State University, USA

"*Activism in Architecture: Bright Dreams of Passive Energy Design* delivers a veritable feast of provocative and timely reading – a mouth-watering menu of contributions from a Pantheon of passive design luminaries. Their insights, structured around the too-obscure work of inventor Harold Hay, cast lenses both scholarly and entertaining, not only on the increasingly critical importance of passive design, but also on the underappreciated revolutionary potential of architecture. I happily share my enthusiasm for these topics – the political and the technical – to entice readers to partake of this delightful new work."

Ann V. Edminster, Green Building Consultant, USA

Contents

Illustrations

Figures

Table

Contributors

Steve Baer is an American inventor and solar and residential designer. He has served on the board of directors of the U.S. Section of the International Solar Energy Society, and on the board of the New Mexico Solar Energy Association. He is the founder, Chairman of the Board, president and Director of Research at Zomeworks Corporation.

Richard (Dick) Bourne is Vice-President of Integrated Comfort, Inc. (ICI). ICI produces cooling efficiency products for buildings. Dick's education includes a BA from Amherst College and mechanical engineering degrees from West Virginia and Stanford. He spent 10 years working and teaching in construction management before moving to California and forming a proprietorship in 1979 that became Davis Energy Group in 1981. After 25 years of leading product development at DEG, Dick joined UC Davis to form the Western Cooling Efficiency Center in 2006. He retired from UCD in 2009 and joined ICI, a 1992 spinoff from DEG, in 2010.

Day Chahroudi has been a physicist at Livermore National Laboratory, and has taught architecture at MIT. He has spent 40 years inventing, building factories for and entrepreneuring products that provide clean energy for buildings. While bringing Low-E and Cloud Gel to the public through Suntek and exploring the profound changes to architecture made possible by these materials, he has practiced many professions, including: physicist, chemist, factory designer and builder, entrepreneur, architect, and structural engineer. He is the designer of some of the best equipment for making the first integrated circuits.

Dale Clifford teaches Comprehensive Design Studios, Digital Fabrication and Professional Practice coursework at the California State Polytechnic University. The vehicle for Clifford's scholarship is prototyping and includes full-scale demonstration projects to field-test responsive building technologies based on regional building practices, biomimetics and material properties. He was a founding member of the UA Emerging Materials Technology Graduate Program, the Bio_Logic Design Group and was a Research Associate at the Carnegie Museum of Natural History.

Dale's research is supported by the National Science Foundation and he has worked on grants and contracts to forward collaborative design research with BuroHappold, IDEO, DARPA, DOE, MIT and NASA. He held a previous appointment with the CMU College of Civil and Environmental Engineering and is a past recipient of the ACSA Creative Achievement Award.

Carolina Dayer, Ph.D is an Assistant Professor in Architecture at Aarhus School of Architecture in Denmark and is the Associate Editor of Design for the *Journal of Architectural Education* in the USA. She is a licensed architect in her native country, Argentina. Her research, teaching and original work centers on theoretical and experimental forms of architectural representation, as well as cultural, political and material practices. She recently published her co-edited book entitled *Confabulations: Storytelling in Architecture* (Routledge).

Kenneth Haggard, an architect in San Luis Obispo, California, was principal investigator of the first full-scale design and evaluation of Harold Hay's roof pond approach to passive design. He is Professor Emeritus at Cal Poly State University and Principal Architect in San Luis Sustainability Group which has designed over 400 passive solar buildings. He is the coauthor of nine books including *The Passive Solar Handbook for California* (1980), *Fractal Architecture, Design for Sustainability* (2006), *Passive Solar Architecture Pocket Reference* (2009) and *Passive Solar Architecture, Heating, Cooling, Ventilation, Day Lighting and More* (2011). He is also author of 54 published papers.

Pablo La Roche is a tenured Professor of Architecture at Cal Poly Pomona University and Sustainable Design leader of the commercial practice at RTKL Associates. He has more than 25 years of experience in professional practice, research and education. Pablo has a professional and a Master's degree in architecture from Universidad del Zulia and a PhD from the University of California Los Angeles. He has authored more than 130 technical papers in journals and conferences and been involved in multiple award-winning projects in the USA, Venezuela, Mexico and Spain. The second edition of his book *Carbon-Neutral Architectural Design* was published by CRC Press in 2016. He chaired the 2016 Passive Low Energy Architecture PLEA conference in Los Angeles and is past president of the Society of Building Science Educators (SBSE) and the solar buildings division of the American Solar Energy Society (ASES).

Margot McDonald has been active in many green-building, renewable-energy and sustainability initiatives related to architectural education and the built environment over the past 20 years as an architecture faculty member and in her current role as department head at Cal Poly, San Luis Obispo. She has worked on a wide range of projects including a consultancy with Sasaki and Associates on a Sustainability Master Plan for California State University, Monterey Bay, and as part of a design-engineering research team that produced a feasibility study for a campus biological solid waste and wastewater treatment facility at Cal Poly. She was the principal investigator for SEDE – the Sustainable Environmental Design Education Program, a curriculum project for landscape and architecture undergraduate professional education funded through the California Integrated Waste Management Board. Her work has been written about in *Ecological Design and Building Schools* (Leibowitz, 2005) and *Women in Green* (Gould and Hosey, 2007). In terms of leadership roles, she has served as chair of numerous committees including Chair of the Board of Directors for the American Solar Energy Society (ASES), chair for the US Green Building Council's Formal Education Committee, and member of the Scientific Advisory Board for Green Advantage. She was appointed representative to the California State University Chancellor's Office Sustainability Advisory Committee for Education and Research and named a system-wide CSU Sustainability Champion for inspiring a generation of sustainability advocates in the built environment.

Daniel J. Overbey, AIA, NCARB, LEED AP, WELL AP is an Assistant Professor of Architecture at Ball State University and the Director of Sustainability for Browning Day Mullins Dierdorf in Indianapolis. His work focuses on high-performance building design and construction, environmental systems research, green building certification services, energy/life-cycle assessment modeling, and resilient design. Prior to his current academic and professional roles, Daniel developed a foundation in applied research focused on environmental control systems through his work at the Center for Maximum Potential Building Systems in Austin, Texas, and the Natural Energies Advanced Technologies Laboratory at the University of Nevada, Las Vegas.

Robert Peña is an Associate Professor in the Department of Architecture at the University of Washington. Teaching and architectural practice have been the means of cultivating and applying the concepts of climate-responsive ecological design to the design studio, to courses in environmental systems for buildings and to professional practice with an emphasis on high-performance buildings. In partnership with the UW Center for Integrated Design, Rob works regionally with design teams on the development of high-performance and net-zero-energy buildings. Since the inception of the Bullitt Center, Rob has worked with the Bullitt Foundation, the Miller Hull Partnership and Schuchart Construction on the design and development of this groundbreaking high-performance building.

John S. Reynolds is interested in how people use energy in buildings, and how buildings shape that energy usage. He has taught both architecture design and environmental control systems at the University of Oregon since 1967. He is co-author of *Mechanical and Electrical Equipment for Buildings*, 6th through 11th editions, published by John Wiley & Sons. A grant from the Graham Foundation for Advanced Studies in the Fine Arts, 1995–6 resulted in his *Courtyards: Aesthetic, Social, and Thermal Delight* (John Wiley & Sons, 2002). He serves on the Board of the non-profit Energy Trust of Oregon, based in Portland.

Susan Roaf (B.A. Hons, A.A. Dipl., Ph.D., ARB, FRIAS) is Professor of Architectural Engineering at Heriot Watt University. An award-winning author, architect, solar energy pioneer and Oxford City Councillor for seven years, her research covers windcatchers and nomadic architecture in Iran, Mesopotamian archaeology, energy, low carbon, resilient and sustainable design and thermal comfort. Famous for building the Oxford Ecohouse in 1995 with the first PV roof in Britain, her books include *Ecohouse: A Design Guide*; *Closing the Loop: Benchmarks for Sustainable Buildings*; *Adapting Buildings and Cities for Climate Change* and the recent trilogy on Adaptive Thermal Comfort written with Fergus Nicol and Michael Humphreys. She is on Boards at the Resilient Design Institute in New York; AES Solar Ltd. and Ecohouse Initiative Ltd. She currently works with the Scottish Government and their Adaptation team, is Chair of ICARB, the Initiative for Carbon Accounting (www. icarb.org), and lectures and teaches internationally.

Vikram Sami has been working on high-performance design for over 18 years, combining technical expertise with a love of design. Since joining Olson Kundig in 2016, Vikram has infused the firm with his infectious curiosity about how buildings can best support the health and well-being of their occupants. Vikram is passionate about working with design teams to help imbue the design process with creative questions about building performance. Vikram's current areas of research include thermal comfort, ventilation, building simulation techniques, carbon reduction techniques and post-occupancy evaluations. Vikram leads the firm's participation on the AIA 2030 Commitment.

William Siembieda applies urban planning principles to the study of resiliency, risk reduction and hazard mitigation. His policy interest is how best to integrate complex public and private actions in the management of resilient and safe urban places. Dr. Siembieda is Professor of City and Regional Planning at California Polytechnic State University, San Luis Obispo, and founding director of the College of Architecture and Environmental Design's Resilient Communities Research Institute (RCRI). Previous academic appointments include the University of New Mexico and the University of California-San Diego and visiting Research Professor at the Disaster Prevention Research Institute, Kyoko University, Japan. Dr. Siembieda holds a Ph.D. in Urban Planning from the University of

California, Los Angeles; and a Master of City Planning and an Economics B.A. from the University of California, Berkeley. He has served as subject matter expert to the World Bank, the Asian Development Bank and the Chilean National Center for Integrated Natural Hazards Management.

Alex Wilson is the founder of BuildingGreen, Inc. in Brattleboro, Vermont, the past executive director (1980–5) of the Northeast Sustainable Energy Association and a former staff member of the New Mexico Solar Energy Association (1978–80). He is currently president of the Resilient Design Institute in Brattleboro, Vermont.

Acknowledgments

This book was made possible through the Trust of Evelyn and Harold R. Hay. The bequest to Cal Poly netted over 200 boxes of source material consisting of correspondence, technical reports, proceedings, and academic papers with a directive to tell Harold's life story which was centered on several themes – none more important than the emergence and evangelism of passive energy design.

Others who knew Harold Hay and contributed indirectly to this story as change agents relaying the importance and ingenuity of passive solar design in buildings include the following people: Ed Mazria (Architecture 2030); GZ Brown (Energy Studies in Buildings Lab, University of Oregon); Alison Kwok (University of Oregon); Walter Grondzik (Ball State University); Murray Milne (Professor Emeritus, UCLA); Harvey Bryan (Arizona State University); Alfredo Fernández-González (University of Nevada, Las Vegas); Mark DeKay (University of Tennessee); Norbert Lechtner (Professor Emeritus, Auburn University); Lisa Heschong (Heschong Mahone Group); Victor Olgyay (RMI); Peter Rumsey, PE; Marty Gluck.

A debt of gratitude is also due to the enduring contributions of the women of the American Solar Energy Society (ASES) including Becky Campbell Howe, Gina Johnson, Brooke Simmons, Pamm McFadden and Maureen McIntyre, who were instrumental in the publications and public outreach efforts through the National Solar Conference proceedings, the National Solar Home tours, and Solar Today magazine. We extend our thanks to Kenneth Haggard, who besides being part of this book was a key figure in early discussions about the project and greatly contributed in framing the first part of the book. Lastly, a special note of appreciation goes to all the authors who made this work possible.

Introduction
Still in haste

Margot McDonald and Carolina Dayer

from this moment
looking at the
clock, I start over ...[1]

Activism, freedom and passive energy design

On April 21, 1970 *The New York Times* published a prelude to an unprecedented event, the very first Earth Day, in which thousands of people were about to march in multiple US cities against the deterioration of the environment. The following day an estimated 20 million mostly young people would march and chant in the streets across multiple cities of the United States. "To make life better" was one of the loudest motivations heard, as reported by the *Times*.[2] What is the significance of this often-proclaimed wish? Perhaps, as American writer Wendell Berry expresses in the poem *Be Still in Haste*, an answer asks for a deeper understanding of the question, one that arrives by re-visiting, over and over again, the meeting and relationship of seemingly contradictory forces.

In general terms, it could be said that the work of activists consists in the formulation of a certain social awareness. Such awareness is often understood as a potentiality to be actualized through changes in policy, new legislation or structural modifications of systemic paradigms. But it is even more than that: one must also possess a thorough knowledge of the chosen subject matter; its behavior, performance and implications. Awareness is founded on a combination of historical consciousness and situational acuity, becoming a powerful tool for speculative projections toward possible future scenarios. Earth Day demonstrations in 1970 were a key moment in history where millions of protesters, headed by Democratic Senator Gaylord Nelson, Republican Representative Pete McCloskey and national organizer Denis Hayes, joined the activist cause of speaking up for the environment. The manifestation directly led to the United States Environmental Protection Agency and to the passage of the Clean Air, Clean Water, and Endangered Species Acts.[3] Several questions can be asked in regard to what extent the protesters were understood as activists. While they clearly support an activist cause, which often contributes to changes being made, is it enough to simply raise awareness? Could activism be understood as a social, political and productive order able to act instead of alert? Should it?

The work of one of the first human-rights supporters in Europe, François-Marie Arouet, known commonly as Voltaire, might offer some insight into these questions. In one of his most well-known works, *Candide*, or *The Optimism*, the French philosopher offers a memorable satire of the Enlightenment's uncritical optimism in the midst of the terrible, everyday miseries of common people. Candide, a protected disciple of Doctor Pangloss, for whom all sufferings happen for the best, sharply deviates by the end of the story from his teacher's absurd optimism. In a somewhat surprising ending, Candide offers a perplexing alternative. In opposition to the suffering of the world, he professes that "we must cultivate our garden," a deceptively simple proposition that leaves one thinking about the agency of personal action.[4] Possibly the first unofficial activist in the modern sense, Voltaire underlines one's personal deeds as a form of action embedded with social and political potential.[5] The action is a presencing of a transformation, but it constitutes also a projection toward a possibility of change.

In her seminal work, *The Human Condition*, Hannah Arendt poses the role of 'actions' as "the only activity that goes on directly between men without the intermediary of things or matter," and thus it "corresponds to the human condition of plurality," which is bounded to the state of all political life.[6] Work and labor, the other two categories concerning the human condition, are connected with such actions' agency.[7] Candide's proposition works at two levels. On the one hand, it declares a position to others – it verbalizes a thought, and thus it acts in the production of meaning and possibly awareness. On the other hand, it proposes a form of acting through cultivation. The verb 'to cultivate' appeals to two forms of action that can be understood pragmatically, as in the cultivation of the garden, and ontologically, as in the cultivation of the self. Arendt suggests that it is in the realm of human action that freedom is attained since it gives us the potential to start something new, to make something unforeseen.[8] To act, then, is to realize that one can be free, and this freedom is connected with political agency. Cultivating the self means cultivating one's larger community as well.

Activism as a creative force proposes also a space for encountering freedom. In the case of the Earth Day march, it was the design and organization of the event led by a group of people concerned with the state of the environment. The event created the space to make visible the beliefs and concerns that would otherwise be invisible. To paraphrase the French philosopher Alain Badiou, an event is a rupture within a given situation, offering the possibility of creating a different condition that challenges a given *status quo*. In this case, the challenge was met through the movement to remedy the environment and the desire to "to make life better."[9] But contrary to the common dictionary definition of activism as "active participation" or "vigorous campaigning," activism emerges also from minor actions and new ways of making, i.e., through inventions.[10] In the case of Berry's *Be Still in Haste*, or Voltaire's *Candide*, it is through the making of poems and fiction that activism opens up a place for thinking and an opportunity for change.

In the context of architecture and environmental activism discussed in this book, the realms of creating and acting are particularly relevant since architecture is rooted, among others, within these actions and their relationship to the environment. Architecture is in fact a key field to instigate a critical discussion of environmental activism through the role of technological ingenuity. Inventions are at the core of architectural design, not as servants of novelty, but as new ways of seeing and seeking potentiality in the actualized world. The history of the word 'invention' in fact does not deal necessarily with novelty, but rather it seeks ways of discovering what may already be there and then re-presenting it in a new way.[11]

By most accounts, architects have always been concerned with the environment, technology and well-being. Already in the first century BCE, Vitruvius wrote that a site's salubrity is a primordial condition in the locus of architecture.[12] By addressing building orientation, quality of air and the need for warmth, coolness and freshness, he continued, the architect should be aware of environmental qualities as actively participating in the architectural design.[13] It is, however, interesting to note that the word 'environment' did not enter the English language as such until the mid-nineteenth century.[14] Technological advancement and the mass production of commodities, building materials and infrastructural systems provoked a colossal shift in the use of the term, which until then had been perceived as being in the middle and center of everything, and not something outside ourselves.[15] In other words, it was a *milieu*, not a specialized or estranged condition. The technological revolution of the nineteenth century not only created this separation, but it came to be the means by which this separation could be flipped inside out. A major demonstration is Joseph Paxton's Crystal Palace, constructed for the 1851 Great Exhibition, where the creation of a 'new' and 'better' environment is made possible thanks to iron and glass technologies. The interiority of the building is conceived as acting separately from the outside, and subject to new methods of control. This was an entirely new concept for large-scale, public buildings.[16] Architecture becomes consciously and technologically empowered with the potential to design environments as self-contained entities.

Since that time, attitudes span from ideas of leaving the building's environment in the hands of specialists and technocrats, to those of architects who continue to design *with* the environment, rather than outside of it. In 1969 Reyner Banham published his pivotal work, *The Architecture of the Well-Tempered Environment*, where he asserted: "the art and business of creating buildings is not divisible into two intellectually separate parts – *structures*, on the one hand, and on the other *mechanical services*."[17] He subsequently exposed what had remained largely undiscussed within the standard histories of modernism focused largely on form and style, revealing how technological inventions have shaped buildings and worked in consonance, or not, with their environment. A few years later, in the field of social sciences, philosopher Ivan Illich argued for a convivial reconstruction of society based on the re-positioning of technology as an autonomous and creative intercourse among people and their environments. For Illich, a convivial society is one that is in control of the tools that shape its everyday life, and this autonomy is what grants freedom.[18] Again, as Arendt had suggested in 1958, freedom is strongly tied to actions that socially and politically connect us to others. Passive energy design, in particular, looks at the design of buildings as already belonging to their surroundings, as environments that interact in the larger web and networks of their context. While it is arguably a continuation of architecture's founded tradition to work with existing local conditions in maximizing building performance, passive energy design has become a formalized field within the discipline that actively differentiates itself from other forms of conceiving and realizing architecture.

This book focuses on the work of architects and thinkers who make the case for a convivial approach to architecture through the innovative use of passive energy design. The included projects and essays position the role of passive inventions as a key form of activism within the field of architecture and environmental control. In contrast to many approaches to sustainable architecture today which treat the environmental impact of buildings as a specialized, technical field outside of its ethical and political implications, this book describes pioneering efforts to link passive energy design with the active political project of advocating for a better, more ethical built world. The book is framed around the work of Harold R. Hay, an American chemist and inventor who strongly believed in the potential of passive energy design and was an activist to its cause. Hay, who was not a licensed architect, was nevertheless a forerunner in environmental design and a leading advocate for the ethical role of architects in relationship to technology, energy and resources. Long before the sustainable energy debates of today, Hay was tackling the enduring question of how to reconcile industrialized building techniques with their impact on society as a whole. Engaged until the end of his long life spanning one hundred years, he continued to write, design and actively defend passive ways of working with energy. His work, although not widely known, influenced hundreds of designers, scientists and scholars who encountered and were inspired by his vision. Hay left a legacy that remains a pillar of activist approaches to passive energy design, acting as a valuable reminder for their fundamental position in architecture while supporting a wide range of current research in the field. He believed that the longer the concepts of passive and active continue to be treated as opposite binaries, the longer we will lack the ability to reckon the potentialities laying within the passive–active structures of reality. This book honors his work and reveals the constellation of authors around it, exposing different positions, questions and thoughts that help us to realize the power of architectural inventions to speak up.

Passive activist: Harold R. Hay

Hay was born on March 30, 1909 in Spokane, Washington. At the age of 27 he filed his first patent consisting of wood preservation, and since then he unceasingly continued to publicly record his inventions until December 22, 2009 when he passed away. Throughout his life he cultivated a voracious curiosity within multiple fields and disciplines. From medicine to ethics, from studies on bezoars and dragons, to chemistry, Hay was an encyclopedic, multi-dimensional figure genuinely fascinated by the history and future of the world. Starting in the 1940s, his work coalesced around the belief that working with the environment's natural energy processes could radically change the world, a conviction he carried until the end of his life. The history of solar energy was for Hay the history of passive technologies that developed primarily through architecture. He alleged, however, that architects were losing contact with the energy performance of their buildings. They no longer designed with energy use in mind, thus leaving the health and efficiency of their edifices to technologically focused systems engineers. He considered this issue not only a problem of design but also an ethical problem of architectural practice. In 1954, still a decade or more before the environmental movement gained momentum, Hay traveled to India where he designed and constructed a small dwelling using his concept of movable insulation. This was the beginning of his most advanced invention, Skytherm, a system that uses ponds of water on roofs and movable insulation to control the storage and release of thermal energy depending on the season and preferences of its inhabitants for radiant heat and coolth (Fig. I.1).

In 1968, Hay and his associate John I. Yellott published an article titled 'International Aspects of Air Conditioning with Movable Insulation' where he carefully explained the successful performance of the system.[19] Beginning to work with architecture in the 1950s, Hay patented his inventions and was active with US government energy policies. A house built in Atascadero, California was the only project in the nation's 1976 bicentennial celebration to receive an award in both categories of environmental and solar energy. It included a citation from President Gerald Ford and a commendation from the American Revolution Bicentennial Commission as an exemplary model of American housing for the next century.

Following his success at the national level, Hay pioneered the notion that passive architecture should play an active role in changing outdated and even harmful government policies. He raised many questions as to why the federal government was reluctant to act upon such a simple and efficacious approach to the built environment. Hay was an activist who believed that it was never too late for ethics. This was his cause and generosity toward the

Figure I.1 Roof pond inventor, Harold R. Hay, seated on the parapet of the Atascadero Skytherm house with architect Ken Haggard (left) and mechanical engineer Phil Niles (right) in 1973.

Source: Photo © Cal Poly Harold R. Hay Archive.

field of architecture – to make and to think with the environment, to act and to speak up, to work and to critique.

Hay frequently highlighted the role of passive energy in previous, pre-industrial societies, seeing this as a valuable source for ethically looking toward future reconciliations with energy use. Inspired by Hay's concerns with the past and the role of ethics in the built environment, this book is organized into three main parts. The model for this structure is motivated by the allegory of Prudence, where looking ahead means simultaneously looking to the present and the past, a foundational concept in Aristotle's *Nicomachean Ethics*.[20] This three-partite structure is then organized chronologically. The first part looks closely at the work of Harold Hay, his writing, the thoughts of his closest peers and collaborators, and their inventions and thinking. Exposing much of their ingenious yet largely unknown built creations, this segment explores the connections between innovations in passive, environmental technologies and how such technologies could play a role in shaping public policy. The second part of the book addresses the work of individuals who were personally influenced by Hay's work in their youth and have since projected his lessons into diverse and realized interpretations. The third and final part focuses on the work of architects who did not meet Hay directly yet whose work is attuned to ideas surrounding passive design architecture and its necessity for a brighter future.

Part I: once upon a sun

Buried within the Harold R. Hay archive at Cal Poly, San Luis Obispo, a curious document by Hay can be found, titled 'Weird, Weirdos and Weird Does.' Its first paragraph declares:

> There were five weirdos in solar energy – now four and aging. All five refused to give up on original ideas that work; all strongly criticized the research of government employees – it was mutual. Their impact on solar acceptance varied from unrecognized great to minor. All were friendly competitors with the common bond of being ignored by those they inspired and helped. Their history must be a part of that of passive solar energy technology which itself is aged and unjustifiably being ignored.[21]

The names of the inventors constituting this group of 'weirdos' were: Harry Thomason, Steve Baer, Day Charoudi, Nick Pine and Hay himself. Three of these provocateurs and ingenious minds form the core contributions of the first part of the book. Through testimonies that expose the spirit of the era and fervent belief in social change, Baer and Charoudi offer strong voices that contextualize not only Hay's work but also their own contributions to the field. Baer's essay, 'Harold Hay's influence and the Zomeworks Corporation,' bluntly lays out his critique of solar electricity and the US Department of Energy's programs while demonstrating the efficiency and creative thinking that was involved in Hay's systems and the experimental wall inventions of Zomeworks. Charoudi's 'Free passive solar heating for cold, cloudy winters' exposes a different constellation of inventions that have their origin at molecular levels. Low-E glazing and Cloud Gel are some of the projects discussed in his essay. This section further includes the work of two architects, Kenneth Haggard and William Siembieda, who personally worked on Hay's projects and contributed to the dream of passive energy design. Because of his deep involvement with Hay's Skytherm project, Haggard makes a double contribution to this book: 'A clear sky story on the evolution of passive solar design,' which focuses on the Skytherm house, and 'The empire strikes back,' which places the project into a larger context as an urban proposal. Taken together, these two essays offer a critical insight into Hay's personality and issues surrounding the discussed projects. Siembieda ends the section with a different perspective on the matter. His essay, 'Determining market demand and feasibility for roof pond systems in California,' shows Hay's effort toward understanding California's residential housing demands in order for Skytherm to become feasible and able to help those who need it the most. This chapter propitiates a clear and larger picture of the context that Hay and other inventors dealt with during their work, and it makes us question such a picture in today's context.

Part I includes a transcribed letter by Harold Hay, published for the first time here, to the Select Committee On Small Business of the United States Senate from 1975. This serves as an introduction to his personal voice and active role in passive energy design. The letter invites us to grasp his passionate dedication for inventions that matter not only for technological progress, but most importantly, for people's well-being.

Part II: active repercussions

Hay once stated, "ideas have a short life in our technology revolution." In a twist of fate, perhaps, Hay's own ideas have enjoyed an unusually lengthy life, many of which have inspired the work of others in diverse and evolutionary ways.[22] Robert Peña compares the work of Hay by introducing an equally activist figure, Denis Hayes, in his 'Creating the context for a solar future.' Peña reflects on two buildings, Hay's Skytherm house in Atascadero and Hayes' Bullitt Center in Seattle, and how these constructions act as concrete forms of activism. John S. Reynolds' essay, 'Shade, mass and water,' focuses on how little is actually necessary to substantially change the conditions of our built environment, particularly when we understand the agency of seemingly minor effects and resources. Courtyards, vegetation and orientation are contextualized socially and historically to narrate their decisive role in the field of passive design. His work is a faithful demonstration of Hay's thought that solar energy has been defeated by solar energy itself, since architects specializing in this field have failed to focus on a holistic approach to passive design. Hay preferred to focus on the natural thermal control of the building space conditioning, or the natural energy flux more broadly considered.[23] On a very different path, but one that convincingly traces the impact of Hay's work and its evolution in the present day, Pablo La Roche contributes 'Passive cooling systems in times of climate change.' Presenting recent scientific research, La Roche reflects upon three projects able to cool through air, sky and water. Two more essays complete this part of the book and they both deal with roof structures directly inspired by Hay's Skytherm project. Richard Bourne's 'Actively stretching passive' examines an alternative system that, instead of working with a large body of water to secure thermal storage, performs with a hybrid assembly of materials that are periodically sprinkled by specifically located hoses. Daniel J. Overbey describes a project by Hay that has not yet been discussed: his Skytherm option for cold climate regions. His essay, 'Untapped potentials in Harold Hay's roof pond system for passive heating in cold climate regions,' not only presents Hay's idea for a roof pond adaptation to other climates, but also offers insightful reflections on its potentials and implications.

Part III: necessity and pleasure

Is there a future in and for passive energy systems? Could they have a role in crafting public policy or building codes? The last portion of the book raises questions about the state of passive systems within the prospect of architecture and the built environment. The essays compiled here examine material explorations, case studies and theories that offer a fresh angle to passive design. Dale Clifford's 'Building experience' looks into questions of new technologies and how they should be paired with a dynamic understanding of the environment. Through an experimental project that performs through phase-change tiles, Clifford emphasizes the importance of an experiential embodiment of architecture as a driver for imagining with new materials and technologies. Susan Roaf's 'Thermal landscaping of buildings' examines why buildings are currently failing and what alternatives could be implemented in a scenario where more frequent environmental catastrophes have begun to adversely affect the life of cities and their citizens. Through various examples, Roaf reflects upon possible strategies that demonstrate new and old modes of active passive design, addressing the need to implement a thermal refuge plan and to elaborate on a natural energy mode for re-thinking building codes. Lastly, the work of an author and a modeler deeply involved within the field of resiliency offers a new outlook on long-lasting, durable design strategies. Alex Wilson's 'Resilience as a driver of passive design' proposes passive survivability as a strategy to incorporate passive energy design into the forefront of architecture. Wilson refers to the vital necessity of adopting such systems if we are going to seriously respond to climatic change and the challenges that come from it. Following Wilson's notion of necessity, Vikram Sami's 'From survivability to thrivability' questions whether, within the many dire predictions of the earth's future, there is still any room in architecture for joy and pleasure. His essay reveals architectural details that are integrated into the building dynamics and engage actively with its inhabitants. Simultaneously these details give room for passive energy performance. This final part of the book offers an open-ended resolution on the topic of passive design and its future by articulating concrete examples of the many directions that it may take. Inspiration through active inventions that take advantage of the intrinsic efficiencies in passive energy is after all what may help us to continue investigating and developing ethical ways to live on a changing planet while employing and ingeniously discovering forms of working with technology and natural systems.

Notes

1 Wendell Berry, 'Be Still in Haste,' *Poetry* 100, #6 (1962): 352.
2 *New York Times*, April 20, 1970.
3 The History of Earth Day, About us, accessed January 11, 2018, www.earthday. org/about/the-history-of-earth-day.
4 Voltaire, Robert M. Adams and Nicholas Cronk (eds.), *Candide or Optimism* (New York: W. W. Norton & Company, 2016).
5 Apparition of the concept of activism as we understand it today, defined by the *Oxford English Dictionary* as "The policy of active participation or engagement in a particular sphere of activity; spec. the use of vigorous campaigning to bring about political or social change," is first recorded in a newspaper in 1920. *OED, Oxford English Dictionary*, accessed January 11, 2018, www.oed.com.
6 Hannah Arendt, *The Human Condition* (Chicago, IL: University of Chicago Press, 2012), 7.
7 Ibid.
8 Ibid.
9 Alain Badiou, Oliver Feltham (translator), *Being and Event* (London: Bloomsbury Academic, 2015).
10 Activism (n.): The policy of active participation or engagement in a particular sphere of activity; spec. the use of vigorous campaigning to bring about political or social change. *OED, Oxford English Dictionary*, accessed January 11, 2018, www.oed.com.
11 Invention etymology: < Latin invent-, participial stem of invenīre to come upon, discover, find out, devise, contrive. *OED, Oxford English Dictionary*, accessed January 11, 2018, www.oed.com.
12 Pollio Vitruvius, Frank S. Granger (translator), *Vitruvius on Architecture* (Cambridge, MA: Harvard University Press, 2002), Book One, Chapter IV, 35–47.
13 Ibid.
14 Trevor Pearce, "From 'circumstances' to 'environment': Herbert Spencer and the origins of the idea of organism–environment interaction," *Studies in History and Philosophy of Biological and Biomedical Sciences* 41 (2010): 241–252.
15 Ibid.
16 Joseph Paxton, *The Cottager's Calendar of Garden Operations* (London: Gardeners' Chronicle Office, 1895); Joseph Paxton, John McKean and Charles Fox, *Crystal Palace: Joseph Paxton and Charles Fox* (London: Phaidon, 1994).
17 Reyner Banham, *The Architecture of the Well-Tempered Environment* (London: Architectural Press, 2009), 11.
18 Ivan Illich, *Tools for Conviviality* (London: Boyars, 1990).
19 Harold R. Hay and John I. Yellott, "International Aspects of Air Conditioning with Movable Insulation," *Solar Energy* 12 (Oxford: Pergamon Press, 1969): 427–438.
20 Aristotle, Robert C. Bartlett and Susan D. Collins (translators), *Aristotle's Nicomachean Ethics* (Chicago, IL: University of Chicago Press, 2011).

21 Harold R. Hay, "Weird, Weirdos, and Weird Does," unpublished document, box 58 (San Luis Obispo, CA: Cal Poly Harold R. Hay Archive, undated).

22 Harold R. Hay, "The Techno/Social History of an Idea: Moveable Insulation," unpublished document, box 92 (San Luis Obispo, CA: Cal Poly Harold R. Hay Archive, undated).

23 Harold R. Hay, "Letter to ISES Solar Weltkongrees 1987, e.V. Hamburg, Attention: Dipl.-Ing. Wallner and Herr Krabbe," unpublished document, box 92 (San Luis Obispo, CA: Cal Poly Harold R. Hay Archive, June 30, 1986).

Part I
Once upon a sun

1 Letter to the Select Committee On Small Business of the United States Senate[1]

Harold R. Hay

Mr. Chairman[2] and Member of the Select Committee:

I am grateful for this opportunity to state an inventor's problem when he works as an individual to help mitigate the energy crisis. A member of the Board of Directors of the International Solar Energy Society, I am author of 20 papers on solar energy and hold 7 patents covering solar processes including solar heating and cooling of buildings.[3] Among past inventions are those of wood preservative and a water purification method in widespread use throughout the world.[4] These contributions had the rewards of "$1 and other valuable considerations" consisting of a salary for a brief period. This is not an uncommon experience among inventors in large companies if they accept the challenge of problems in other fields instead of sinecure advancement to administrative positions.

The purpose of this statement is to outline chronologically the development of an invention which the General Electric Company characterized more than a year ago as follows: "Conceptually, the Skytherm house would appear to be an ideally simple, inherently straightforward, and particularly appropriate use of the nature energies of solar radiation and night-sky cooling." Other commendatory comments on the simplicity and breakthrough aspects of the system will be found in the attachment.

In 1953, during the HUD[5] foreign assignment in India, I conceived and proved new principles for economic solar heating and cooling of buildings; the invention was not welcomed by foreign aid officials unfamiliar with research. The successful tests, however, gave me an absolute faith in the invention along with the realization that there would be no acceptance of the principles until after their adoption in advanced countries.

For 17 years, top "planners" and "administrators" of the AID,[6] HUD, the UN,[7] and other agencies were repeatedly reminded of the systems but they were certain that simple solutions were too difficult, and it was easier to hope that nuclear energy would supply all future energy needs. The late Professor Farrington Daniels and Professor John I. Yellott were the two sources of encouragement among solar experts; others suggested that I go back to chemistry. The two professors well deserve their status as pioneers and impartial evaluators in the field of solar energy.

In 1972, Mr. Orville Lea, of HUD, intelligently broke the pattern in government and said the time had come to study a system such as mine: as an architect, he appreciated its adaptability to low-cost housing. A too small ($35,000) project was approved by the HUD for a team of eight California Polytechnic State University (San Luis Obispo) professors, with Kenneth L. Haggard as principal investigator, to evaluate a Skytherm house built with my private funds. The project conformed to the proposal in ex-President Nixon's Science Message to Congress for an inventor of a pollution-free energy source to collaborate with a university to use federal funds to develop the invention. I know of no other successful project along these lines; yet, in the early stages, it was dropped and reinstated (under pressure) within two working days. Subsequent delays in contract processing, difficulties in obtaining minor additional funds, and refusal of a $15,000 extension to redesign the house with correction found advisable during prototype testing and to obtain new cost estimates as well as calculations on performance improvement stopped progress in bringing the successfully demonstrated system onto the market. HUD was not to blame entirely, since jurisdiction for solar energy development had passed to NSF.[8]

The 1972 NSF/NASA Solar Energy Panel's report "Solar Energy as a National Energy Resource" was a self-serving program that misled Congress by not mentioning systems already proved with funds of individual inventors (Dr. Harry Thomason, the writer, and others). It stated incorrectly that solar systems are capital intensive (some are, some are not – the generalization condemns all), and so convinced Congress, the FEA,[9] other agencies, and the public that solar heating would require 3 years for demonstration, and solar cooling 5 years, although systems not advocated by the panel merited immediate demonstration. The program bore the seeming intent of "Research Forever!" After 3 years, the NSF systems have not yet reached the promised demonstration stage; Congress did well in removing responsibility for solar energy development from NSF – unfortunately, in 1975, the NSF personnel transferred almost en masse to the new agency (ERDA)[10] given solar energy jurisdiction. Faulty policies remained in effect.

In 1973, the Atascadero Skytherm house established its outstanding success; the final (January 1975) evaluation report describes it as "a unique and invaluable national and worldwide asset." The professors found that it can do what no other system claims – 100% heating and 100% cooling without use of gas or oil and only an insignificant amount of power with resulting comfort "far superior" to gas heating. The professors, moreover, found that the system was much more economic than other solar systems and that, in mass production, the first cost of a Skytherm house might be no more, possibly less, than one conventionally built with installed heating and cooling systems. An expectation that ERDA and HUD would widely publicize these results has not been fulfilled in the past ten months; publicity continues to pour out of ERDA saying that solar heating and cooling is far off. For example, three generalizations that are untrue in relation to Skytherm appear in four consecutive sentences on page 41 of the Erda-48 document "A National Plan for Energy Research, Development & Demonstration: Creating Energy Choices for the Future":

> Efficient solar cooling systems which operate with low quality heat do not yet exist. Improved coatings and collector materials which are environmentally resistant would improve the performance of solar systems. Current means of integrating solar systems into existing and new structures are too costly. The high initial cost of solar heated and cooled houses overshadows potential life-cycle costs.

Skytherm is an efficient solar cooling system within the definition in Section 3 of PF 93–409 that governs ERDA operations; it operated with low-quality heat to produce a comfort superior to "high-quality" heat. ERDA should stop referring to solar heat as "low quality" if it wants public acceptance. Skytherm is not "too expensive" to integrate into existing and new structure of certain types and it does not have a high initial cost. Constant repetition of defeative [sic] statements by federal officials retards public acceptance of Skytherm and other successful systems.

Since 1972, NSF (and, for 7 months, ERDA) has looked indifferently on Skytherm accomplishments and refused invitations to visit the house or to discuss the results. Worse, the scientific principles and data were ignored, it literally took force to get mention of passive systems and nocturnal cooling. NSF funded big industry (TRW, Westinghouse, and GE)[11] to propose new concepts and a general plan for their development. Heavily funded with about $500,000 each, the companies came up with no new concepts but, instead, produced plans adding old and complex technology to overcomplicated and conventional equipment. This approach adds so much cost that the companies could not predict substantial market penetration before the year 2000. Residential use had to be played down; passive systems and nocturnal radiation were ignored by TRW and Westinghouse though both knew of them. GE was more attentive to all systems but did not recommend simple ones for further study. Congressional pressure caused NSF and ERDA to reconsider these studies under the excuse that rising utility rates present a new picture, but the rising rates had been predicted as part of the Phase 0 reports.

Dr. Lloyd Herwig, in Denver, and Mr. Ray Fields, in Phoenix, both NSF policy-making officials at the time, stated that solar research was not being studied in the Southwest because in effect it was too easy; but they did not say what method could stop the waste of gas and oil in the Southwest where solar energy use is easiest. As if to sabotage solar energy, large, uneconomic projects were concentrated in areas of minimum feasibility to serve as "sideshows" to relieve political pressure for faster action. Discussing reasons for not stating a position on or supporting the Harold Hay system,

Dr. Herwig included the uncalled for remark, "As I understand it, Harold's life has not been completely trouble-free either up to this point." Dr. Herwig had been informed privately by me that I had been McCarthyed and cleared in 1954; the fact that he recalled this and made a public reference to it implies in my opinion that this had been a factor in an adverse NSF attitude toward my projects.

Other than the fact that NSF took a position to ignore passive and proved systems, four projects dealing with my system were refused funding:

1. The Cal Poly professors had a project designed to continue research on the Skytherm house and system turned down.
2. The Rand Corp., of Santa Monica, was not funded for a study said to have been submitted to determine the cost of the Atascadero house and its potential impact on energy conservation.
3. A small project, in which I proposed to apply my principle to very low-cost housing for American minorities and people in developing countries, was, in my opinion, blackballed – two reviewers gave the project good grades, the third graded it so low that it could not have been accepted if the other graded it 100.
4. After Dr. Eggers, head of the NSF solar program, personally promised to fund a project to have a large, architectural engineering firm make an independent study of the results of the Atascadero house, to determine specifications and costs, and to determine its applicability to a variety of buildings and locations within applicable climate of the Southwest. The project was rejected by Mr. Fields after an agreement had been reached with the largest A/E firm on the Pacific Coast that they would submit it if NSF was interested. It may be significant that Mr. Fields, a former employee of Westinghouse, was aware that I had very severely criticized the Westinghouse Phase 0 report. That Mr. Fields may not have a viewpoint free from past associations is indicated by his reply to my recommendation that NSF publish a map of the United States that would show areas where no air conditioning is required, where nocturnal radiation and evaporation can economically reduce peakload power demand, and where conventional air conditioning is fully justifiable because of condition of high humidity. Mr. Field replied that it would not be politically wise to publish such a map. One would prefer a more scientific response from officials of the National Science Foundation.

After ERDA based its first "National Plan for Solar Heating and Cooling" (March 1975) on the NSF/NASA panel report and on Phase 0 studies, several persons criticized it for continuing to ignore the passive and proved systems. The revised document (ERDA 23a, issued October 1975) is vastly improved, shows far better understanding of building technology, and gives rather adequate attention to passive systems, nocturnal cooling, the role of small business, and even mention of the individual. A major objection that I raised to prior policy must be repeated here because the unchanged policy is most unfair to presently economic systems such as Skyther. The Cal Poly professors have reported that in mass production Skyther may cost no more than conventional heating and cooling in a custom-built house; General Electric, in its Phase 0 study, stated, "The basic materials and design aspects (of Skytherm) should support the low cost potential claimed." Yet in ERDA 23a, and in the implementation thereof under HUD's "Request for Grant Application H-2353" for residential demonstrations and in the policy is "Federal funding for demonstrations will have an upper limit of the amount by which the cost of a building with a solar system exceeds the cost of a similar building with only a conventional heating and cooling system." This policy subsidizes high-cost and uneconomic systems; it denies subsidy to a system economic now and it minimizes help to any nearing this desirable goal. Once more, this is a policy harmful to the development of solar energy; it would be better to set a subsidy of a given amount – say $5,000 – and let the achiever of a lower-cost system have a reward that will help him attract financing for production and that will give the producer of a high-cost system partial encouragement but notice that his costs will have to be reduced.

Almost as discouraging as this policy on subsidies is the statement in PON DSE-75-2[12] that, "The primary interest at this time is for space heating and hot water systems. Responses dealing with combined solar heating and cooling will be considered, however future PON's will specifically address the combined systems." This policy again hits a method such as Skytherm which accomplishes both heating and cooling now. The "hurt" is that this method will receive no credit for accomplishing the goal of combined heating and cooling years before ERDA will subsidize such systems. ERDA's words that solar cooling "will be considered" do not suggest that it would be wise for a builder to look around for a system that will do both; he can get a very large subsidy without doing so. The builders have repeatedly been told that solar cooling is uneconomic now; ERDA 23a repeats 13 times the theme of increased cost for solar heating and cooling without intimating that one system does not have high costs.

To indicate how damaging this negative attitude of NSF and ERDA has been, there is attached a photocopy of a story about Skytherm that was given 2/3 of a page in the Business Section of the Sunday Los Angeles Times (circulation 1.25 million). Not one businessman responded to enquire about opportunities to participate in Skytherm development – nor even to look at the house! Federal officials have conditioned the minds of businessmen against early investment in solar energy; this on top of the extreme shortage of venture capital and a depressed housing market has made it impossible for Skytherm to start commercial production. An inventor has problems after he succeeds in developing "a unique and invaluable national and world-wide asset." It is a truism that new ideas go through three stages: ignored, opposed, and accepted. Generally speaking, Skytherm is not yet at the stage of being openly opposed.

Skytherm is finding some parties willing to apply for HUD grants and ERDA contracts for the heating and cooling demonstrations. Many more parties would surely have indicated interest if ERDA had given early publicity to the new passive systems instead of concentrating on the old, high-cost systems. Also, it is pertinent that the HUD application for a grant is far simpler for a small businessman to submit that is the ERDA application for a contract. There are many commercial buildings smaller than the condominiums and garden apartments in the HUD program, but the high cost of meeting the elaborate ERDA application requirements will preclude submission of small projects and encourage subsidy of large ones. Again, ERDA policy discourages the very small business interests from involvement in solar energy.

As recommendations to this Select Committee, I should like to submit the following:

1. FEA should be encouraged to make an immediate study of the marketing problems of small businessmen and of inventors who have ready-to-go solar heating and cooling systems. FEA is already authorized to study constraints and incentives that apply to this problem and has shown a greater concern about the daily waste of energy resulting from slow introduction of solar energy than has ERDA.

2. ERDA should promptly issue a contract to a competent architectural engineering firm for a study of all solar energy systems now claimed to be economic and ready for commercialization. The resulting report should indicate constraints and advantages of each system for different types of buildings in different climates and should estimate their market penetration potential as well as the energy conservation that should be obtained through their early demonstration. Skytherm is ready for such a comparison but there has yet to be the first serious enquiry from a federal agency about the cost of applying Skytherm on one of its new buildings.

3. ERDA (for commercial buildings) and HUD (for residential ones) should be advised to emphasize the early installation of side-by-side demonstrations of all solar energy systems claiming to be economic in any region of the country. An early report on the cost and performance of the systems can save billions of dollars that will otherwise be wasted in buildings being completed daily with a requirement for gas, oil or electricity during the next 40 years or more.

4. The NSF and ERDA should be asked to broaden their support of small business to include programs specifically for creative individuals.

5. ERDA and HUD, as well as DoD and other federal agencies involved in new construction, should be advised to give preference to solar systems that are economic and can do both heating and cooling now.

I wish to commend this committee for its concern about the part small business can play in the commercialization of solar energy. Inventors working alone are expressly grateful for any concern by Congress that will lead to opportunities for him to help solve our serious energy problems.

Notes

1 All endnotes by the editors.

   In 1940, the USA Senate created the "Special Committee to Study and Survey Problems of Small Business Enterprises." This committee was terminated in 1949 but in 1950 the "Select Committee on Small Business" was established to continue with the previous committee's functions. The select committee was once again terminated to become a standing Committee on Small Business. In 2001, Senator John F. Kerry renamed it "Committee on Small Business and Entrepreneurship" and it is still functioning today. U.S. Senate Committee on Small Business and Entrepreneurship, About, accessed on February 24, 2018, www.sbc.senate.gov/public/index.cfm/history.

2 In 1975, the chairman of the select committee was Gaylord Nelson, U.S. Senator and governor of Wisconsin and the founder of Earth Day in 1970.

3 Process and apparatus for modulating temperatures within enclosures: US3903958A, US Grant (1957), US3299589A, US Grant (1965), US3450192A, US Grant (1967), US3563305A, US Grant (1969), US4089916A, US Grant (1975); Process and apparatus for solar distillation: US3314862A, US Grant (1965), US4055473A, US Grant (1974). Hay's last patent on the Skytherm roof system was filed in 2002 as Process and apparatus for modulating temperatures in thermal storage: US6827081B2, US Grant.

4 Purification of Raw Waters: US2444774A, US Grant (1943), Inventor Harold R. Hay, Current Assignee: PQ Corp; Wood Preservation Patent #US2209970A, US Grant (1936), Inventor Harold R. Hay, Current Assignee: Monsanto Chemicals Ltd Monsanto Chemical Co.

5 HUD: U.S. Department of Housing and Urban Development.

6 AID: United States Agency for International Development.

7 UN: United Nations.

8 NSF: National Science Foundation.

9 FEA: Federal Enterprise Architecture.

10 ERDA: Energy Research and Development Administration.

11 TRW: Thompson Ramo Wooldridge was an American global supplier of automotive systems, modules and components to automotive original equipment manufacturers and other related aftermarkets. A German company, ZF Friedrichshafen, bought TWR in 2005 and it is now called ZF TWR Automotive Holdings Corp. GE: General Electric.

12 PON: Program Opportunity Notice. The Commercial Solar Heating and Cooling Demonstration Program at Marshall Space Flight Center was initiated by the predecessor of the current United States Department of Energy (DOE) in October 1975, with the release of the first of four yearly Program Opportunity Notices. Robert L. Middleton, "The Solar Heating and Cooling Commercial Demonstration Program at Marshall Space Flight Center – Some Problems and Conclusions," *The Space Congress Proceedings* (April 1, 1978). The

specific PON Hay refers to in this letter is the DSE-75-2. Energy Research and Development Administration, Division of Solar Energy, *Proceedings of Pre-Submission Conference on Program Opportunity Announcement, DSE-75-1, and Program Opportunity Notice, DSE-75-2* (Washington, DC: Energy Research and Development Administration, Division of Solar Energy, 1975).

2 A clear sky story on the evolution of passive solar design

The source and multiple applications of Harold Hay's roof pond system

Kenneth Haggard

Complex and difficult characteristics often appear to be key ingredients in the personalities of great geniuses. Harold Hay, the godfather of passive solar design, was no exception. This chapter seeks to critically expose, from personally working with him, the philosophy, conceptual basis and contradictions of Hay's attitude toward research, invention and application. From the visionary idealism and potential simplicity of the roof pond concept to the concreteness of the Atascadero, California prototype, Hay is credited with the only solar building in the nation able to provide full cooling and heating data during the 1973 oil embargo crisis.

While Hay's background was in chemistry, he was essentially an integrationist. He seemed to be able to cross most disciplinary boundaries at will. This trait served him well as an inventor. He also had the ability to piece divergent aspects of a situation into a unified concept. As with most of the classic inventors, he had faith in his creations as well as an intense stubbornness to push for and defend his concepts.

Particularly, Hay was fascinated by the biological response to climate and solar radiation. He was fond of saying that for biological materials such as hair and skin, "white is hot and black is cool." Curious in comparing his physical features as a person of Scandinavian descent to that of Africans south of the Sahara, he was incessantly interested in how our bodies perform in different sun regimes. The Swedes like him evolved in a sun-scarce climate and need solar-induced vitamin D. He claimed his long, straight, white hair acted as a fiber optic, bringing sunlight to the lower levels of skin similar to polar bears with their white translucent fur above their black skin. Conversely, African people exposed to a climate of solar excess would have black hair to absorb sunlight at their tips, re-radiating that energy away from their heads. The air trapped in their curly hair acts as insulation. Hay claimed to be the only person who could explain to dermatologists sunburn on lower cells of the skin in certain northern latitudes, as well as the Tuareg people's preference for black woolen tents in the hot Sahara desert.

Solar radiation 'inwards' during the day, and earth radiation 'outwards' during the night, was another of Hay's big interests. He believed the two working together could be used to provide both heating and cooling for buildings. In the bigger picture Hay was evangelical in regard to the world's chance to replace fossil and nuclear fuels with solar energy. His first name was a perfect fit for his efforts. He and his devoted wife Evelyn felt he was a prophet, heralding an approach toward energy that would save the world.

I met Harold in 1971 at California Polytechnic State University, San Luis Obispo (Cal Poly). It was through an introduction by Ben Polk, a well-known architect who had a large practice in India before settling into semi-retirement as a professor at Cal Poly. He had met Hay when he was a building materials advisor to the government of India in the 1960s. It was during this time that Hay was directly impressed with the 'white is hot' phenomenon. Working outdoors with building materials in the hot Indian climate, plus his discovery of the Yakhchāl ancient Persian constructions able to produce ice in a hot desert by night sky radiation, were some of the sources that contributed to his later inventions.

The experiences during this trip stimulated Hay's concerns of coupling high-mass materials, movable insulation and night sky radiation. Upon his return to the United States, he experimented with trays of water exposed at night and covered them during the day to cool, and conversely he exposed the water during the day and covered it at night to heat. Based on these principles, he then developed a system that would provide natural air conditioning and heating for buildings, which he labeled Skytherm and which was patented in 1969. Subsequently the Skytherm system of heating and cooling was successfully tested through an experimental cell at Professor John Yellott's solar laboratory in Phoenix, Arizona.[1] Simultaneously, Hay was looking to create a team of people to take Skytherm one step further with a highly integrated full-scale house. This is when I met him. The full-size test was to be evaluated with a promised grant from the United States Department of Housing and Urban Development (HUD). Polk's introduction to me came with a warning: "It makes me cold under the eyeballs thinking of working with Harold," a statement that I, of course, ignored but later understood all too well.

As an idealistic assistant professor, I was enthusiastically attracted to Hay's philosophy of saving the world and his program to build a solar building. This project promised to be not just a test cell, but a fully functioning building inhabited by real people. Hay stipulated a system where the whole edifice was to be evaluated in eight areas: architecture, methodology, construction, movable insulation, automation, thermal, occupancy and economic evaluations. He was also adamant that the building and its components would cost no more than a typical suburban house of the period. His Skytherm concept was to be evaluated in a seamless, interdisciplinary manner. Hay was an integrationist above all else and I was too young and inexperienced to know how difficult this task could become.

After I was assigned to put together a team, we developed the grant proposal for $40,000 to HUD for the evaluation work. The design of the building was done by Cal Poly Architectural Engineering professor John Edminston and myself (Fig. 2.1). Hay agreed to pay for the building costs

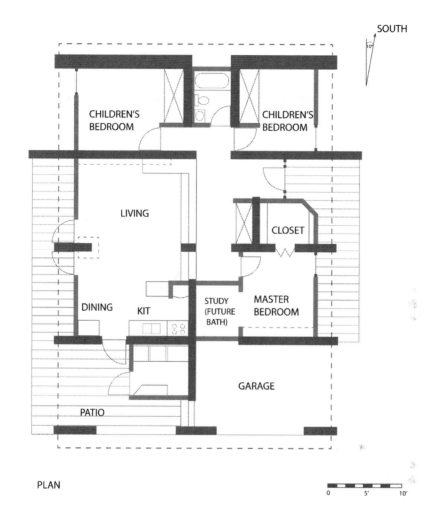

SOUTH

CHILDREN'S
BEDROOM

CHILDREN'S
BEDROOM

LIVING

CLOSET

DINING   KIT

STUDY
(FUTURE
BATH)

MASTER
BEDROOM

GARAGE

PATIO

PLAN

0   5'   10'

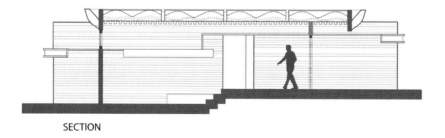

SECTION

Figure 2.1 Plan and section of the Skytherm Atascadero house.
Source: Drawings by author.

using a small inheritance from his recently deceased brother. After some studies of alternative sites, we selected a location in Atascadero, which was close enough to the university campus. The selected area was located where the heating and cooling loads would be much greater than at the milder coastal climate of San Luis Obispo.

Over the next six months, we designed a system of 4'x12' movable insulation panels that could be stacked three deep in the open position. The movable panels would open and close over a deep roof structure containing water bags to propitiate enough thermal mass. Jake Feldman, our structural engineering team member and Cal Poly professor, built and tested a system of three full-scale movable insulation panels and operating them until failure. Then, a redesigning phase would focus on the failed part. Through this way of working and testing, we were able to iteratively develop a system of movable insulation at the size required to cover the entire roof. The final dimensions were 4–12'x8' panels, which would create a 36'x40' system of movable insulation on the roof, stacked three deep on an adjacent 8'x12' roof space (Fig. 2.2 Above).

Phil Niles, our thermal evaluator and mechanical engineering professor at Cal Poly, developed a computer prediction model of the system, which showed that in this climate we would need an insulating air cell over the ponds to prevent excess heat loss from the ponds. This model, CALPOND, was probably the first performance model for passive buildings anywhere.[2] Afterwards we did the working drawings, acquired the building permit for the house up through the metal deck roof and contracted with a local builder to construct the dwelling upon which we would later add the ponds and water bags, movable insulation system and automation devices.

The building was very simple. It consisted of five parallel 8" concrete block walls spaced at 12' 0" spanned by a 3"-deep prefabricated metal deck. Concrete block lintels allowed opening within the walls as needed to serve a three-bedrooms-and-two-baths dwelling. The lot sloped east to west, which allowed a split level inside that gave a 10'-0"-high ceiling to the living room, dining room and kitchen and an 8'-0" ceiling to the rest of the house (Fig. 2.1).

At the start of construction we concentrated on installing an elaborate instrumentation system consisting of thermocouples and thermistors to provide data for good thermal evaluation once the building was in operation. By this time, Niles had also developed an automation system that would allow the opening and closing of the roof's insulation system. This option was an optimized version of pulling a rope twice a day that Hay had done on a previous test cell in Arizona. Niles' system involved using a differential thermostat and a tiny test cell sensor mounted on the roof to compare the desires of the occupants to the performance of the roof if the panels were open using a differential thermostat. The problem, however, was that at this time, no differential appropriate thermostats were available for the task. Niles had met an enterprising electrical engineer, Robert Schlesenger, at a conference,

Figure 2.2 Above: Harold Hay stands beside the Phoenix Prototype test structure
in 1967. Below: Atascadero Prototype House with insulation open and
with insulation closed.

Source: Photos by author.

who agreed to design and make a prototype for our project. He subsequently
went on to create a firm, Rho Sigma, producing these devices just in time to
become the basic supplier during the soon-to-arrive passive solar movement.

Once construction was nearly finished, we were ready to install the roof
ponds, movable insulation and automation systems. However, prototype
problems emerged. We were destined to learn what was actually involved
with full-scale prototypes. One of the issues was that the water bags creating
the roof ponds had pinhole leaks. The plastic manufacturing limitations of
the time made it difficult to create polyethylene cells without this short-
coming. In addition, attempts to create the required air cell above the ponds
using Hay's solar still designs from previous projects proved to be too susceptible to flutter caused by high wind speeds often occurring over flat

roofs. Experiencing the ecology of a flat roof over the seasons is an experience few people get. The accentuation of wind speed as mentioned, but also the prominence of heat and cold due to solar and night sky radiation, are very much like desert conditions. Furthermore, water generates particular condensation conditions that can produce self-starting siphoning in track beams and other devious behavior. There is also a surprising amount of organic material found in flat roofs like bird feces, insect bodies, leaves, dirt, pollen, etc.

Besides prototype problems, we started discovering how Hay was susceptible to extreme mood swings, which made consistent efforts more difficult than what we had hoped. In fact, at times this behavior was threatening to the entire project. Polk's warning words started to become more vivid. Dealing with these problems caused delays and we needed the building to start operating soon so we could collect data, otherwise we could lose the winter testing season.

In desperation, we finally resorted to more expensive polyvinyl chloride water bed technology for the roof pond cells, much to Hay's chagrin, since he was against this material because it was more expensive than polyethylene and its manufacturing process more toxic. However, this allowed double glazing by adding an air bubble on the surface of the resulting four 8'-0" by 40'-0"-long waterbeds serving as roof ponds. As usual, Hay was ahead of the curve.[3] Finally, the test period got underway on February 5, 1973. We were well into taking data when America's first energy crisis arrived with the oil embargo crisis of 1973.

The United States was extremely vulnerable to this situation. As a country we were happily cruising along with a huge inventory of highly inefficient automobiles. We had neglected our railroads to move most freight by trucks, and had created post-war suburban sprawl with almost total dependency on private vehicles. At the same time we had become more and more dependent on cheap oil from the Middle East as our own easy-to-produce wells became depleted. Suddenly, the lifeblood of this whole construct was drastically reduced. The system started shutting down. There were long lines everywhere at gasoline stations trying to get fuel that was in many places unavailable. Tempers became short, fights at gas stations started occurring and rationing was initiated in many places. For me this time was highly auspicious. I was involved in this solar project because I was critical of the aesthetics of closed, air-conditioned buildings, but now something much more concerning was occurring.

Suddenly perceptions about our research project changed from a small group of eccentric assistant professors working for a crazy inventor to far-seeing celebrities. A wave of publicity on the house and its continuing performance was mounted. It was a very heady time. We were on European television programs, interviewed by hosts of reporters, and had a large spread in the *LA Times* newspaper and a six-page article with flashy photos in the *House Beautiful* magazine, which had a whole issue on the promise of solar buildings exemplified by the Skytherm approach. Not concerned with fame, Hay was more interested in fully testing Skytherm and urged us to publish scientific papers on the work.

The evaluations on Skytherm were completed in 1974 and a final report was sent to HUD, which was published by the National Technical Information Service as 'Research Evaluation of a System of Natural Air Conditioning' in January 1975. The thermal evaluation was particularly well received. True to Niles' modeling, the interior temperatures were extraordinarily steady due to the 30 tons of water on the roof radiatively coupled to the interior. The inexpensive cost of water, 12 dollars from the tap, plus its high heat capacity made it the most effective material for passive applications. Most people expected some heating success as a solar building, but the cooling was generally a surprise and easier to accomplish in this climate. Most of the many visitors at this time, even those who did not really understand the technical basis of the house, commented upon the uniquely positive feeling of the interior in regard to comfort. This was due to the massive radiant transfer of heat and coolness provided in the different seasons (Fig. 2.3). Within all the excitement of success, we started to think about the future. We imagined that in five years we could stand in any southwestern American suburb in the early morning and watch seas of roofs open their movable insulation in unison with the sunrise in the winter. A promising vision, but in hindsight we were still amazingly naive.

The house received its formal debut at the Solar World Conference held in the summer of 1975 at UCLA where Hay, Niles and I presented papers. Hay's presentation was on the Skytherm concept, Niles' on the modeling and mine was on its architectural implications. My impression from the conference was that the Solar Energy Society at the time was composed mostly of a collection of eccentric scientists and tinkerers amused at the idea of solar energy but not expectant of much practicality. Solar energy was a project of potentialities, not of realizations. My paper was the only one specifically involving architecture and was the last paper presented at some far corner of the campus. Nevertheless the eccentrics and tinkerers, possibly out of curiosity, showed up in force for my presentation. The only other related activities were ad hoc rump sessions being held in the student union on the unheard subject of appropriate technology instigated by Steve Baer and a few other "outlaw designers." In two short years "outlaw design" was to become a rallying cry for a large hipper segment of the rapidly birthed passive solar movement.

This movement was formally born in 1976 when Doug Balcomb, a nuclear physicist in Los Alamos Labs, organized the first passive solar conference in Albuquerque, New Mexico.[4] Attendance was expected to be several hundred people, and over 500 showed up. Suddenly we realized we were not the only ones doing passive solar research and design. It was interesting to see how many nuclear physicists were involved in those early days. Frightened of nuclear power, they were anxious to find productive alternatives. Balcomb

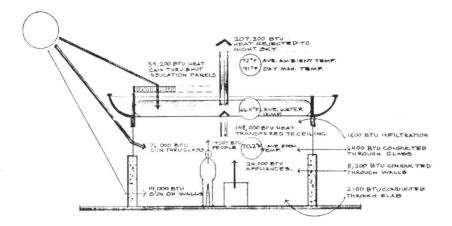

TYPICAL DAILY ENERGY TRANSFERS IN HEATING MODE FEB. 18, 1974

TYPICAL DAILY ENERGY TRANFERS IN COOLING MODE AUGUST 1974

Figure 2.3 Thermal flows of the house in typical winter and typical summer periods. Source: Diagrams by author.

and Niles working on computer modeling, and Don Aiken with day lighting, were nuclear physicists who did much of this valuable early work.

Soon after in 1977, the Federal Government organized an invitational study meeting of most of the passive designers and thinkers, funded by the Department of Energy. This was held at a conference center in Reston, Virginia, far enough from Washington DC to minimize distractions for a weeklong effort. There was a lack of a formally agreed-upon theoretical framework so at times that these meetings resembled a tower of 'babble.'

It was here that Niles and I met Marshal Hunt and David Bainbridge. There were two recent graduate students from the University of California, and Davis who had done a lot of solar energy work including the Davis Energy Plan.[5] They had also worked on Michael and Judy Corbett's Village Homes, the first passive solar subdivision in the country, and had designed and built a roof pond house while working at the solar design firm of Living Systems for Jonathan Hammond. At this point Hunt and Bainbridge were the technical staff for the newly formed California Energy Commission and were interested in developing a passive solar handbook for California. We arranged a two-hour escape from Reston by hiring a taxi to take us out for pizzas and beer, making a deal that the handbook would be completed by Niles and me using Energy Commission funding. Things were looking up! There was enough money in the contract to work on the project and even buy some time from the university, so we could dedicate ourselves to work without the need of teaching full time as we had done with the Atascadero prototype.

The development of numerical modeling of passive systems by Niles for this Passive Solar Handbook resulted in CalPas 1, which then became California's public domain building energy performance model.[6] It later evolved into CalPas2 and CalPas3. This modeling allowed side-by-side comparisons of different passive architectural applications, which were published in the handbook. Roof ponds generally outperformed other approaches. They were less reliant on temperature swings for their operation, less limited by south orientation and more comfortable due to their large thermal mass. We thought Hay would be very pleased with our comparative analysis of different passive systems, since it honored and scientifically clarified the success of his idea, but this was hardly the case. At first he fought the handbook and its publicity for reasons we never understood. Only later he accepted the handbook's content and used it to publicize his Skytherm system.

Hay also explored adaptations of roof ponds to other climate conditions, allowing the expansion of his system to serve more severe climates.[7] Subsequent work by the Atascadero Prototype team also expanded the roof pond approach beyond single buildings in 1977 with a 'new urbanism' roof pond design for California.[8]

Hay lived to be 101 years old, remaining very committed to passive design until the end of his life. From the point of view of many of us who worked with him, however, he never succeeded in taking the next logical step in the development of Skytherm. Our team always felt that this next step could have been a thorough industrial design development of the entire system. This would have avoided each roof pond project to become another prototype and would have allowed increased efficiency of production. However, Hay remained skeptical of who could be right for such an undertaking.

While on one hand he wanted Skytherm to be taken seriously, on the other hand he sought full control of the system and was too concerned with letting it go. Though he became a wealthy man late in life by investments in the stock market and could have easily funded such an effort, he instead spent his last years funding university studies and general research, as well as fighting the Department of Energy who he felt did not appreciate his approach to passive solar design.

The Federal Department of Energy did eventually fund a technical review of all the Skytherm work. The aerospace company Rockwell International was in charge of this effort.[9] While a thorough review of work done to date, it did not deal with what would have been the logical next step after successful prototypes. Its values as a summary without any emphasis on evolution made it as much an epitaph as a step forward.

In 2004 Alfredo Fernández-González, an architecture professor working with polyethylene roof pond test cells at Ball State University who later moved to the University of Nevada in Las Vegas, developed a proposal and funding for an extension of Skytherm in the form of a pavilion. Hay rebuffed González' project in much the same way he had done to our comparative studies of passive systems in the *Passive Solar Handbook for California*. Consequently, a proper industrial design development of such a promising system as proven by successful prototypes has yet to be done. In the end, Hay remains to me a great mystery, an enigma consisting of extremely committed scientific rationality as well as righteous emotional irrationality. He had an intense desire for a massive worldwide application of his concepts, and yet an unwillingness to release enough control so the project could be developed with the help of others.

This chapter has exposed the recollection of essential material relevant to not only understand Hay's invention and great contribution to the field of passive energy, but also to uncover a clear sky for the evolution of the roof pond approach now that Skytherm's patents have expired.[10]

Notes

1 John Yellott was professor of mechanical engineering at Arizona State University and one of the few people in the country at the time experienced in solar heating for buildings.
2 Philip W. B. Niles and Kenneth L. Haggard, *Passive Solar Handbook* (Sacramento, CA: California Energy Commission, 1980), 312–313.
3 Later work by Alfredo González at Ball State University and the University of Nevada at Las Vegas indicated that polyethylene cells could eventually be manufactured leak-free at a very reasonable cost. González has published widely around this theme; see for example: Alfredo Fernández González, "Defining the Optimum Dimensions of Test-cells to Research Thermal Comfort in Passive Solar Buildings: A Direct Comparison Study," Proceedings of the SOLAR 2003 Conference, Austin, TX (June 2003): 581–586.

4 J. Douglas Balcomb is the author of the book *Passive Solar Buildings*, published by Cambridge, MA: MIT Press in 1992, among other key works in the field of solar design.

5 The first community plan in the country achieving energy conservation policies and regulations.

6 Philip W. B. Niles and Kenneth L. Haggard, *Passive Solar Handbook* (Sacramento, CA: California Energy Commission, 1980).

7 Skytherm north design for the Midwest and upper Great Plains using roof ponds in the form of solar attics with movable insulation shutters on south-facing attic roofs.

8 New urbanism as an architectural movement began around 1980 as a reaction to the problems of suburban controlled planning and the dominance of the automobile. It recognized some of the advantages of pre-World War 2 planning such as grid street patterns, alleys and mixed use. A Skytherm version of a new urban design project is described in Chapter 5 of this volume.

9 Why fund this type of study by a defense industry without philosophical interest or experience with passive solar applications? It was our perception that the Reagan Administration trusted aerospace firms more than solar professionals or professors. Such perception was based on the fact that one of Reagan's first acts in office in 1980 was to gut the national Solar Energy Research Institute and to remove the solar panels that his predecessor President Carter had installed on the White House.

10 Hay's roof pond patents issued around 1969: no. 3,299,589, no. 3,450,192 and no. 3,563,305.

3 Harold Hay's influence and the Zomeworks Corporation

Steve Baer

False flag methods mark the renewable energy revolution. Like our false flag wars with false foes, we move toward false goals. The deception is the same: solar electricity on the grid is substituted for freedom from the grid. More than forty-five years ago, Harold Hay led efforts to heat and cool buildings without utilities. This has been replaced by others waving the solar flag but working for utilities and wealthy tax evaders. Self-reliance, independence and conservation are replaced by over-consumption and US Department of Energy programs. Instead, Hay built prototypes of inexpensive buildings heated and cooled passively. Today our establishment avoids such answers and promotes subsidized solar power plants and wind generators to feed their electric grid.

I first met Hay in October 1968, at the Palo Alto, California International Solar Energy conference. We sat on wooden chairs in the motel conference room. Harold towered over us: six feet four inches tall, black suit, black briefcase, white hair. He emphatically presented slides of John Yellott's and his successful Skytherm experiments in Phoenix. A roof pond covered in day time, uncovered at night, cooled the building all summer. Inversely, it kept the dwelling warm during the winter. Unfortunately, the Skytherm heating and cooling system has gone nowhere. In the United States, we have too few buildings passively heated and cooled. A modern green militia, building solar electric, guards the solar alternative. It is the old game at work: "heads they win, tails you lose." Hay and Skytherm never had a chance – not conservation, not passive solar, not off-grid "making do" where possible. In its place, we have a helpless dependence on the grid. Hay's rages from forty years ago, frequently interrupting conferences and meetings, have been replaced with "professional" gobbledy-gook and technical reports. Instead of designers and builders struggling with climates, it has become easier to merely switch meanings, where solar energy equates solar electricity. Will the press and green "radicals" repeat this endlessly? While subsidized solar power plants and wind generators continue to help the 1%, designers and developers forget that the sun is hot and the sky is cold, relying on complicated pumps and devices to attain heat and coolness. The absence of Skytherm, Hay's vision and built prototype, is not surprising, nor is the lack of support for clothes lines, bicycles or carefully oriented windows. These familiar solar marvels offer no kickbacks – does this explain their absence from the green vision? Hay's easily outraged personality had moved "off-grid" before we were familiar with this opportunity or had developed inexpensive photovoltaics. Passive and off-grid systems are now possible for all. This is recognized by a culture fearful of fossil fuels which insists that solar passive design impersonates habits developed using them. The memory of Hay, an outspoken advocate for the citizen and passive solar design, does not fit with today's obsession with solar electricity.

Our work at Zomeworks has centered on extending the work of Hay and other solar pioneers, such as the solar prophet Farrington Daniels, founder of the International Solar Energy Society and Hay's chemistry professor in the 1930s at the University of Wisconsin. After working on the Manhattan Project, Daniels was rebuffed by the Atomic Energy Commission.[1] He then devoted himself to the "poor man's fusion reactor" – the sun. Zomeworks is based on their philosophies and has been dedicated to creating passive solar products to help achieve their vision. Unfortunately, Drum Walls, Bead Walls, Sky Lids, Sun Benders and other passive products along with Hay's Skytherm have been largely abandoned to favor state subsidies and green propaganda for renewable electricity grid power.

A neglected slice of the building market currently sustains Zomeworks. These are passively cooled batteries and equipment shelters, which are ignored by green activists. Unfashionable engineers purchase these Cool Cells because they are simple and reliable. Cool Cells have allowed us to continue innovating Hay's vision since 1989. They consist in highly insulated, passively cooled, outdoor enclosures that protect and prolong the life of batteries and low-power electronic equipment. The night radiation cabinets are conceived purely from Hay's inventiveness, even breaking his rules to fulfill his vision, for we let water move at night. A plenum cabinet lid cools water at night flowing to a plastic tank within the cabinet.

Waters maximum density at 39 °F stops thermosiphon flow without a valve at about 45 °F. Water's massive heat of fusion, 144 BTU/lb along with a maximum density at 39 °F, guards against overcooling. We found water eager to live in a Cool Cell since it knows when to flow and when not, when to cool and when to heat, based on this interesting physics principle. Selling these around the world has whetted our appetite to make altered Skytherm systems as double-play structures, which break additional passive rules for the use of PV-powered pumps.[2]

Hay's inspiring beginning with Skytherm was necessary but has not yet proven sufficient. That is the job of those who follow, to keep evolving the potentials of an idea. We can create tools and equipment that extend our use of the sun and can provide liberty and freedom instead of dependence on government hierarchies and power grids. In such a spirit, this testimony describes a work that originated after meeting Harold Hay.

Alternatives to movable insulation

Panels that move and insulate, covering and uncovering a naked thermal mass such as a fifty-five-gallon drum or a roof pond, are difficult to make. We have never been able to do this at Zomeworks. But is movable insulation necessary? Without movable insulation, Hay's ambitions can still be met and inexpensive passive heated and cooled dwellings are possible. The problem with movable insulation is air leaks through gaps and cracks. While gaps can be controlled initially, aging, sagging and creeping eventually occur in such mechanisms. To reach Hay's vision of passive cooling using water, we started with the same principles but contradicted his methods. Another significant issue in Hay's roof pond system were the water bags that, while inexpensive, were plagued by failures as they do not thrive in resisting pressure. Zomeworks' idea, while discouraged by Hay's dramatic personality, was to move away from the movable panel and to construct a well-insulated roof with a radiator above it. Instead of opening a panel for cooling, water runs through the radiator at night. In both systems, Cool Cells and double-play structures, circulating water moves through natural convection. To employ thermosiphon cooling one needs the radiator above the water, thus some slight pressure. These trivial concerns are of great consequence and solving them occurs "off stage." In our Cool Cell cabinets we successfully use roto-molded polyethylene tanks. However, in initial buildings we have unfortunately used poorly optimized overhead large-diameter PVC irrigation pipes. Could these tanks be blow-molded polyethylene rather than toxic PVC? Thus far we have not attracted money for the molds and prototypes Hay's dreams deserve.

Skytherm and drum walls

After hearing Hay in Palo Alto in October 1968, I built a large insulated box containing a fifty-five-gallon steel drum of water behind a single glazed glass pane. A reflector door facing south hinged at the bottom, which I opened every day and closed at night – it worked. Even during the 1971 cold snap when temperatures dropped below zero, the box and its drum stayed above 70 °F. After the successful test I built a house (Zome cluster) employing the same heating system (Fig. 3.1). I truncated the four southernmost Zomes – exploded rhombic dodecahedra – and placed walls of steel drums on their sides in a locking rack of angled iron. Each drum had a south-facing wall of 24"x24", a single-strength glass panel. The fifty-five-gallon drum created a thermal mass of at least 120 lbs of water per square foot. Often, the system temperature fluctuated at 10 °F, gaining and losing enormous amounts of heat. However, while its heating performance was successful, cooling by opening the door at night and closing it during the day did very little.

Time passed and details failed. Despite an application of corrosion inhibitor, the drums leaked, so in 1991 we redid the Hay-inspired drum wall.

Figure 3.1 Above: Exterior of zome house showing drum wall and movable insulation panel, 1970, Zomeworks Corporation; Below: Interior of zome house showing drum walls, 1970, Zomeworks Corporation.

Source: Photographs by author.

Dave Harrison, who worked at Zomeworks for years, replaced the ninety steel drums on their sides with sixty polyethylene upright drums that have not leaked since then. The glazing façade is now an acrylic exolite double wall and new reflective doors are left open all winter and closed all summer. The changes and renovation have proved that the system works without the need for insulated doors.

Harold and I stayed in touch for the rest of his life. He remained a passionate advocate for passive solar design and water in polyethylene bags. In this regard, Harrison recommended the use of vinyl instead, but Hay thought we were not using the right polyethylene, and he wanted to keep experimenting with the material to better optimize it. Tank liner people who use urethane brought Hay to a rage, and he never mellowed. At almost one hundred years old, he was a session chair at the National Solar Conference in San Diego, CA. He was still sharp, and although he could no longer bring order with a booming voice, he tinkled his glass of water with a spoon. It worked.

In his last years he considered a project of adding extra thermal mass to dwellings – bags of water – to smooth out hot afternoons and cool mornings; these could be located under beds, for example. True for most of California, Governor Jerry Brown understands the importance of passive energy design and encouraged such projects in the 1970s, such as the Gregory Bateson building by Sim van der Ryn in Sacramento. Why aren't projects like this or Hay's Skytherm more common? Who but Hay would support them?

Fools dismissed the ancient crackpot Harold Hay. His critics still do not understand that his intentions could hardly be met in one project or even a lifetime. His desire was to contribute to a civilization, not to a bank account. Why else would Hay labor so much to make sure that non-Department of Energy projects, such as those of Harry Thomason and Zomeworks, were discussed at meetings?[3]

Hay's influence had more to do with his character than anything technical. He was dedicated to something we have not yet reached. Sitting beside this frail old man at the last Denver Solar Conference, I could have been beside a tractor trailer, not a wheelchair, for his moral power.

Visits with him always left impressions. Staying with us one winter evening, Hay first had a whiskey and read through the *Wall Street Journal*. He had investments and had turned a small inheritance from his wife into much money. He took chances and bought on margin. He also had profit and nonprofit organizations and claimed that making a fortune was easy. Easy for him, not so easy for others. Hay's mind worked all kinds of ways – to make money, to find puns, to invent. That same evening Hay called me to the bedroom to show me what he had done with the cushions from the sofa bed. "Movable" insulation, he called them. They were placed in front of the windows.

Such movable insulation was less difficult than one on top of a roof filled with water bags: inside, cracks and gaps are not so treacherous;

Figure 3.2 Hammond's bead wall movable insulation system, 2017.
Source: Photograph by author.

outside, winds and large pressure differences do not cause rapid air flow. At Zomeworks we did not succeed in using outside panels as first attempted by Skytherm, but we did succeed by using a bead wall, another movable insulation system invented by Dave Harrison in the 1970s (Fig. 3.2). Bead Wall has been Zomeworks' most startling product. Styrofoam beads are blown in and sucked out of a two- or three-inch space between glazing. There are no air leaks and the insulation value on winter nights is indeed R3 per inch. In summer, the beads block the sun, which does nothing more than glow through them.

We should remember this unpublished success. Today, forty years later, Harrison heats his house through a huge bead wall that he recently refitted with new fiberglass glazing, while keeping the same beads. We faltered in promoting the bead wall largely because of mistaken distress for a lost patent. In the 1970s we sold many, at least a thousand licenses for people to build their own bead walls, and many fiberglass bead storage tanks with vacuum cleaner motors. All this happened while we believed we had a patent. Then we received bad news: the Japanese had used a bead wall in a greenhouse earlier. No more patent, no more license, no more plans. The fate of the bead wall became similar to Hay's Skytherm – victims of subsidized competitors.

One must accept enthusiasm for new computers and cell phones but not false flag solar. Grassroots solar lost its flag to tax-supported, big-money solar power plants and wind generators. If this wasn't bad enough, such competition has also shriveled the old solar grassroots. This is what the bead wall and Skytherm have been facing. If only Hay could have lived even longer, making his way to Washington DC in his wheelchair, asking questions and writing letters. A great advantage we have today, which Hay did not in 1975, is the infrared scanner. These inexpensive pistol-grip thermometers allow us to see what Hay saw magically with nothing; surface temperatures day and night. Why is the roof of a car 10 °F below ambient temperature at night? Why 60 °F above in the day?

I can see no end in the dispute between technology and culture. Hay was a leader in working with this – he was devoted to technical details previously mentioned here, but he was no nerd. He came from an age before there was a faith that technology can determine all of our built environment. Perhaps this was associated with his enormous size and strength. What to make of the story of youthful retaliation to a logger's antagonism? He believed in right and wrong, not "might makes right," and he often repeated: "the bigger they are, the harder they fall." What comforted me working with Harold was his courage and innocence; never a bully.

Hay was not perfect. On my first day knowing him, I heard about a special joint in his arm that allowed him to pat himself on the back. Which he did. To me, this hero of Western culture mistakenly transferred a youthful, well-earned faith in corporate engineering managers, who later developed his early ideas, to department heads at universities who did not. In fact, the genius of Hay anticipated universities solving these problems when universities specialize in not even noticing them. What is wrong with private enterprise? Those of us in business following his lead were never able to get the backing he bestowed on universities. Perhaps this book will bring his ideas and character some of the attention they deserve.

False flag propaganda and subsidies pretend solar energy is like scarce fossil fuel, but it is not. It is free. Along with the make-believe world of subsidies and propaganda is the real world which Harold Hay and Farrington Daniels saw and which today beckons us off-grid, using better and cheaper PV panels, better, cheaper selective surfaces, appropriate low-e windows, batteries, insulation and the essential infrared scanners and temp recorders.

Who needs a subsidy to build a miracle? Instead of being discouraged or defeated by fossil fuel hangover or even the present misguided energy subsidies, think how Hay and Daniels did it. Ours is a new age. Uncounted advantages support an enlightened society fed up with deception, with treasonable leaders who belong in a museum of dead ends. We have straightened things out before and we can again. What wonders can be done even with war surplus from misguided energy wars?

Corrupted powers fear the uncorrupted. How can they bribe the honest? How can they bribe you? An off-grid energy-conserving community would upset the plans of entire industries. This is behind the subsidized misuse of renewable energy. Indeed: no power plants, no enormous new transmission lines, no trucks bringing out-of-season vegetables.

Notes

1 The Manhattan Project was the top-secret government project that developed the atomic bomb toward the end of World War Two.
2 Buildings using double-play structures do solar heating and night sky radiation cooling, but unlike Hay's Skytherm system, they use separate elements for each function, essentially moving the water rather than moving the insulation.
3 Harry Thomason was a lawyer from Washington DC and was an early solar inventor for the Trickle Collector, a very simple, inexpensive, but efficient solar heating system.

4 Free passive solar heating for cold, cloudy winters

Designing molecules and crystal structures

Day Chahroudi

In 1967, I was working as a physicist at Livermore National Laboratory in Berkeley, California where the USA's nuclear bombs are designed. Gandhi was one of my father's heroes, and is one of mine as well. Therefore, I took this job on the basis that I would not be working on nuclear weapons. When I found out they had lied, I quit, despairing of using my scientific skills to benefit people. Disillusioned like so many young people of the time, my wife and I hitchhiked to New Mexico in 1969, which was at the time a hotbed of alternative lifestyles.[1] On the way, we learnt about the technical work on passive solar buildings being done by Steve Baer at Zomeworks Corp. I met Steve at Corrales N.M. and he made an unrefusable offer: working on solar heating buildings for $40 per week, the same amount Livermore was paying me per hour.

Steve had an elegant design aesthetic that I shared, which is uncompromising simplicity. He explained the importance of infrared radiation in heat transfer in buildings and introduced me to his inspirational teacher, the chemist, Harold Hay. Harold explained that the amount of energy a building receives on its surface is three times as much as is used inside of it. As a materials scientist, I had my work cut out: simply make a building's outside surface out of the right molecules and crystal structures to capture and control that energy. Since heating uses about 65 percent of a building's energy, two materials needed invention: first, transparent insulation to let sunlight into a building while keeping its heat from escaping, and second, a glazing material that when heated would reflect sunlight away from the building to keep it from overheating in the summer. Joseph Paxton's Crystal Palace for the first World's Fair in London in 1851 and Buckminster Fuller's transparent geodesic dome for the United States pavilion in the World's Fair in Montreal in 1967 are examples of the desire to enclose spaces with transparent structures. These two projects, as spectacular as they were, could not fully control the climate of the spaces they enclosed. The work at Zomeworks, discussions with Hay and reading the research of Maria Telkes[2] convinced me that fundamental materials design was needed to extend passive solar heating to the cold, cloudy winters where most heating energy is consumed.

Working at Zomeworks, I had key realizations thanks to Hay's inventions. Baer's house was his version of Hay's Skytherm, consisting of large insulating doors which acted as a solar reflector during the day and insulators at night to retain the heat. It was Hay's system made into a south wall. As a materials scientist, it occurred to me that if there was a material that was both transparent and also insulating, the design would be more beautiful, with no moving parts. A transparent insulation that collects solar heat in the winter would make a solar oven in the summer, so a second glazing material would be required: one that reflects sunlight when it is warm. This would perform like the second function of Baer's insulation doors: rejecting unwanted solar heat.

In 1971, I received $2,000 to further develop the research. I spent the next year living in my station wagon parked outside the Library of Congress researching materials that could perform as transparent insulation and thermo-optical shutters. Physics theory said that very thin coating of silver is the best material for transmitting light and reflecting infrared radiation. But the silver had to be only 50 atoms thick for high light transmission. One hundred and sixty scientific papers explained that in order for a silver coating to form a continuous layer with low light absorption, it had to be at least 10,000 atoms thick. Using atomic psychology, I realized that the silver had to be coated onto a transparent material so that the silver atoms would think it was actual silver. Indium oxide proved to be the best such material, so low-emissivity (Low-E) coating was born: 50 atoms of silver sandwiched between two indium oxide layers. The vibration of its electrons tuned to transmit light but reflect heat made windows that insulate like walls and roofs, heating buildings with the scant light from cloudy skies – even in freezing weather! I made the earliest samples of Low-E glazing materials in 1972 (they transmitted sunlight and reflected infrared heat very well, but had durability problems).

Serendipitously, I stumbled across a polymeric material that is soluble in cold water, but precipitates out of solution in hot water, like a heated egg white. But, unlike egg white, this polymer goes back into solution and turns clear again when cooled. I then had to design a polymer molecule that could precipitate at room temperature, and is not further degraded by sunlight. This thermo-optical shutter glazing became "Cloud Gel." I documented this effort in U.S. patent 3,953,110, and many succeeding international patents.

Unknown to me at this time, the cold war was proceeding in a way that would directly affect me. The Russians were bathing the American embassy in Moscow with microwave radiation to charge up their bugs and for deleterious health effects to embassy staff. Protecting U.S. embassies is the responsibility of the CIA. Steve asked if the material I was working on to reflect infrared radiation heat would also block microwaves. It was an odd question for two reasons: to a physicist, the answer was obviously yes, so why ask; and second, what do microwaves have to do with solar heating? It was then that Steve invited some visitors ("potential funders") from Sandia Lab who had asked about my work.

After the intensive literature research on Low-E glazing, I returned to Zomeworks to continue my work developing test samples in 1972. The two threads of this story joined in 1973, when Sean Wellesley-Miller from MIT drove out to Albuquerque. At that time 80 percent of MIT's budget came from the military. "Coincidentally," Wellesley-Miller said he had submitted a proposal to the National Science Foundation to study solar heating buildings with a hypothetical transparent insulation and a hypothetical optical shutter. They turned him down, saying such materials could not exist. When he showed them the Low-E and Cloud Gel samples I had developed, they offered the grant and I had a job at MIT. I was not to learn of the CIA's interest in Low-E until 1984, when I read in a newspaper that the first use of Low-E glazing was at the U.S. embassy in Moscow to block microwaves.

While a faculty member and researcher at MIT, I felt the development of Low-E glazing was successful enough to be completed in the private sector. Money was becoming more available from the Carter Administration for solar heating, so I wrangled a $100,000 grant from the Department of Energy and formed a R&D company, Suntek, in the Silicon Valley area. The choice of location was fortuitous, positioning us a few miles away from the company that made all the world's glass-coating factories: Airco Temescal. Their research director/production manager, Bob Cormia, joined Suntek because he found Low-E intellectually stimulating and valued my uncompromising design aesthetics. This beauty is the only thing that the best and brightest scientists care about. A few years before, Bob had invented the coating technology that we selected to produce Low-E.

In order to keep the somewhat antagonistic cultures of R&D and manufacturing/marketing separate, I formed a new company, Southwall Technologies, to build a production machine and sell Low-E, selecting their senior staff and giving them the patent rights to Low-E and the machine I invented to make it. Paul Mellon was reputed in 1989 to be the richest person in the U.S. Unknown to me, he held a controlling interest in Gulf oil and was a founder of the CIA. His daughter offered to invest $5 million to start Southwall Technologies. What more could a naive solar "goldilocks" ask for? In 1991, the Mellons did a hostile takeover of Southwall Technologies, Suntek was history and I was broke.

It is normal for inventors to be cheated of the rewards of their first invention, but if it is profitable, usually they can easily raise capital for their second invention under fair terms. So, I could hope that the birth of Low-E glazing would be successful enough that investors would remember how profitable it was (Southwall Technologies went public for $65 million six years after its $5 million startup investment). Further, Low-E glazing saved consumers $8 trillion in heating bills because it became the standard glazing for buildings. Low-E's rapid global market saturation came from the glass industry; Southwall Technologies captured only 0.5 percent of the non-CIA market. It chose not to defend my patents, which they owned, on Low-E materials, production process and machinery. Given free rein from my patents, the glass industry eventually spent about $2 billion building Low-E factories. This was the inventor's dream, but earned me not a penny.

Uniting inventions: Weather Panel

It is helpful and rewarding to compare the architectural concept implied by the inventions that originated from Harold Hay's roof pond passive heating and cooling concept. "Weather Panel," a component that emerged from uniting Low-E and Cloud Gel glazing and a three-inch layer of non-circulating water, is a product directly connected to our mentor (Fig. 4.1).

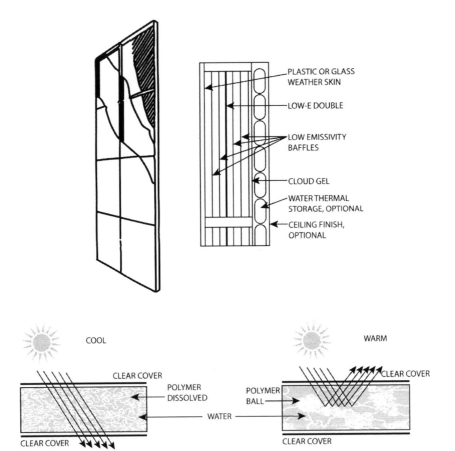

Figure 4.1 Above: Weather Panel cross-section, Below: Cloud Gel performance diagram.
Source: Drawings by author.

These are not solar heating panels that sit on top of a roof like a flat plate heat collector or photoelectric panel. Like Hay's roof pond Weather Panels became the roof. Their performance was a translation of Hay's roof pond system. The mechanical design performing through moving insulation was replaced with molecular design performing through transparent insulation and thermo-optical shutter glazing. The moving parts are molecules and electrons rather than bulky insulating panels. But the system is clearly a direct transformation of Harold, Steve and Maria's elegantly simple and overlapping concepts. Unlike Hay's roof ponds, Weather Panels do not cool with night sky radiation, which fits their market of solar heating in cold, cloudy and humid climates. Their properties today are:

- Solar absorption or transmission which varies from 4 to 50 percent, depending on the building's needs for heat or light
- Thermal resistance of R10 sq ft (degrees Fahrenheit) hr/BTU, or 1.75 sq M (degrees Celsius/Watt)
- Installed cost $25 per square foot (E250 per square meter)
- Optional overnight heat storage in a 2-inch (5-cm)-thick-layer water or nanotech chase change thermal storage
- Either translucent for illumination, or with an interior ceiling finish for heating
- Self-cleaning, low-friction outdoor surface for snow removal
- Fireproof due to water heat storage
- Lifetime of 40 years

Because Weather Panels were designed for bad weather, they heat with the light from cloudy skies, which comes from all directions. Thus, the shape of a roof does not affect the amount of light it collects, so a Weather Panel roof does not change a building's design; except it has a 45-degree slope for snow to slide off.

Low-E earned each of the glass manufacturers billions of dollars and hundreds of millions of dollars in profits, but the fact that I invented and founded Southwall Technologies gave me entree to the company's Research Directors, Presidents and Board rooms. For evaluation of the Weather Panel concept we chose the Belgian glass manufacturer Saint-Roch. They spent $1.5 million to evaluate a solar heating roof made with Low-E and Cloud Gel, shared equally between Suntek for making the roof, the European Union for field-testing it in a building and internally at Saint-Roch for evaluating Cloud Gel performance, building their own model production line and building a full-size demonstration.

The test building near Brussels has the same cold and cloudy winters as Boston, Paris and Tokyo – weather that consumes the most heating energy. During the January and February test period, there was no direct sunlight, so the above performance was achieved with the light from clouds alone! While the performance of previous solar heating designs had always been below 50 percent, the Weather Panel roof's heating was 85 percent solar.

These test results show that one-sixth of the world's energy is available at no cost by collecting cloud light with roofs using molecular design, placed precisely at the pivot point of a global energy flow.

Massive success of Low-E glazing and a missed opportunity

Low-E glazing has achieved almost universal application. It costs only $.04/ sq ft, and enough has been manufactured to cover the entire state of Rhode Island. To date, it is estimated to have saved $8 trillion worldwide in heating costs, has reduced CO_2 production to the atmosphere by 2 percent and saved 3.4 million lives by reducing fossil fuel pollution. Low-E glazing saves twice the energy of all solar cells, testifying to the importance of energy conservation. It was brought to market for only $6 million for a cost-benefit ratio of 1.3 million to one, making Suntek by far the most effective clean energy organization.

As important as energy conservation is, Low-E glazing has energy production capabilities as well. Its early conception was for passive space heating gains, but this has been lost due to its great success in the conservation of energy. However, it is possible to vary the solar heat gain characteristics of Low-E films. The inherent conservatism and simple-minded marketing strategies of the glass commodity manufacturers, as well as the general ignorance of many architects, result in the loss of this passive solar aspect of Low-E glazing. It is difficult to find window companies to supply Low-E glazing with high solar heating coefficients for passive solar heating – which requires coating low-iron glass with a silver layer only 50 atoms thick, much thinner than is optimal for energy-conserving (rather than collecting) windows.

Development of Cloud Gel thermo-optical shutter

As dark as things were in the world of big oil and big money, there were bright horizons on the clean energy front. I sold the $3.2 million that I had in Southwall Technologies stock to resurrect Suntek in Albuquerque, New Mexico. Our mission was to develop and produce Cloud Gel, the glazing material that is a necessary partner to Low-E for solar heating roofs. Cloud Gel is clear and transmits sunlight when it is cool and heat is needed. But when heated, its molecules change shape and turn white. This reflects away sunlight when a room is too warm, working like a thermostat. Cloud Gel is clouds when you want them.

Technically, Cloud Gel's weakest point was degradation by sunlight. My extensive literature search showed that Michael Heskins had done the best work on sunlight-degrading plastics.[3] He was to Cloud Gel what Bob Cormia was to Low-E: absolutely essential. Like Cormia's decision to work on Low-E, Heskins was attracted to the scientific beauty of Cloud Gel.

We exhausted my little fortune to build two factories: one to make the Cloud Gel polymer, and another to laminate that polymer between two plastic films. By 1989, we had developed a process for making Cloud Gel from commercially available materials and the finished product, a laminated plastic film, had passed accelerated-aging tests. In only two years, we designed and built two factories, developed and optimized two processes for them, and, from accelerated-aging tests, developed a marketable product. As when Suntek was developing Low-E, we had a talented staff of critical mass. Reuniting Low-E glazing for collecting solar heat and reducing heat loss with Cloud Gel for modulating heat gain could allow us finally to create climate envelopes that produce the energy they consume.[4]

The urgent necessity for free clean energy

Our industrial culture is based on evolutionary change; consequently, it has also created rapid and severe climate change. For survival, our adaptation must also become much more rapid and effective. Failure of imagination and courage in the financial community have delayed for decades the marketing of Weather Panels – a clean, free source for one-sixth of the world's energy. Bringing Suntek's huge source of free, clean energy to the world has been sabotaged by the then richest man in the world: Paul Mellon, a CIA founder who also controlled Gulf oil. This sabotage has speculatively increased global warming by about 10 percent, taken 300 million years from our lives and has cost us $10 trillion of unnecessary energy bills.

Those of us who practice passive solar design and other architects must start working with passive energy design and already existing inventions. At Suntek, we have been squeezing the beautiful Low-E technology into the cracks in an ugly global money machine, prostituting a source for one-sixth of world energy from solar heating in exchange for windows that conserve a mere 3.7 percent of world energy. Nature will increase our pain via climatic disruption and its catastrophic effects of fires, hurricanes, floods, droughts, famine, refugees and war until we get it and choose correctly. Free clean energy as an integral part of our built environment is the choice we must make for our culture and our bodies to survive the world change we are making.

Notes

1 New Mexico was a uniquely rich contrasting mix of American Indian culture, "hippy" alternative organizations like the Lama Foundation, Zomeworks Corp. and the military weapons labs like Los Alamos and Sandia that were part of the government's atomic weapons builders. Zomeworks and Sandia weapon labs were in close proximity and interacted occasionally in regard to technological ideas.
2 Maria Telkes, *Solar Still Construction* (Washington, DC: U.S. Dept. of the Interior, 1959).

3 Michael Heskins, *Energy Exchange in Polymers* (PhD Dissertation, University of Toronto, 1969).

4 The aptly named Eden Project in England consists of eight transparent domes, each with a different climate, covering 125 acres (or 50 hectares). They contain 4,000 trees, bushes, herbs, crops and flowers that are most useful to humans. The project designers were eager to use Low-E and Cloud Gel, but I very foolishly declined their interest because their plastic film dome did not fit our chosen market entry point for Cloud Gel: the centralized, high-capital glass industry that had rapidly saturated world markets with Low-E.

   Though they need their own power plant for heating and cooling, the lush Eden domes show what it would be like inside a "Climate Envelope." Cloud Gel with different clouding temperatures could create such various climates.

5 The empire strikes back

When too good becomes threatening

Kenneth Haggard

The late 1970s was a period of almost giddy optimism for passive solar design. Successful prototypes had been constructed and evaluated; President Jimmy Carter and Jerry Brown, the youngest governor in California's history, were both solar advocates. Federal and state money was available for research and conferences. Prediction modeling was becoming available through the work of Phil Niles and Doug Balcomb via the federal Solar Energy Research Institute. Special products were being developed and marketed such as movable shutters, movable insulation and reflectors by Zomeworks Corporation, specialized glazing and water storage tubes by Kalwall Corporation, and solar water heaters superior to any today.[1] Many of these products coming onto the market in 1979 are ironically absent 40 years later. Other examples were: phase-change thermal storage material in sealed cans, sticky-back selective surface material for Trombe walls and Bainbridge walls.[2]

After the stifling administration of Ronald Reagan, Jerry Brown appointed Sim Van der Ryn as the State Architect, one of the most outspoken of the "outlaw designers" who was very ecologically oriented.[3] Governor Reagan's philosophy had been for the state to rent office space from the private sector so there was a shortage of state-owned offices in the capital area of Sacramento. Under the new administration it was decided that new buildings for the state should exemplify the new approach to energy conservation via solar buildings. The first step was to propose a competition for a new State Energy Efficient Office Building to be held in two phases. Phase one consisted of a general first round where several submissions would then be selected for a second round with some development funding for further elaboration.

Some of the team members involved in the Atascadero roof pond prototype, Phil Niles, Jake Feldman and me, with the blessings of Harold Hay decided to develop a roof pond entry for the competition. We saw this as an opportunity to extend Hay's unique system to an urban scale at a greater density than the suburban-type house in Atascadero. We started this effort with a trip to Sacramento to see and study existing state office buildings in the area around the competition site. The urban pattern of central Sacramento is one of a Midwest-type grid pattern, consisting of wide streets lined with mature street trees and ample sidewalks as well as low-rise buildings. Once there, we started to examine the existing site's immediate context. We visited all state office buildings close by, studied their plans and form, and interviewed as many people as we could who worked in them.

We found that there was a definite evolution of these buildings from the oldest built in 1923 to the most recent at the time, built in 1969. Together they were almost like a cartoon of a 50-year-old slice of architectural history. They were extraordinarily clear in their progression from Eclecticism through Art Deco; Classic Early Modernist, "Radiant City"-type slab and two Mies van der Rohe-like office towers (Fig. 5.1). From our interviews we found that people who worked in these newer buildings were not very happy about them. General comments were that they were too large, too cut

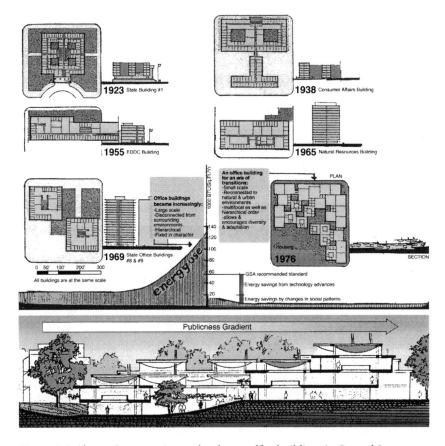

Figure 5.1 Above: Comparative study of state office buildings in Central Sacramento; Below: Site section with publicness gradient from grid pattern of streets.

Source: Drawings by author.

off from the outside environment and in spite of the dominance of central mechanical systems, noisy and with uncomfortable temperature swings.

It became evident that the newer the building, the more cut off the occupants were from the surroundings, the urban pattern and the outside environment. We wanted to reverse this situation. Our concept was that the new office building should recognize and relate to the urban pattern of Sacramento like the oldest 1923 building that housed the governor and his staff. We also preferred the smaller-scale office suites that existed in this building before the advent of the high-rise "office landscape" pattern of the 1960s. This earlier scale of office clusters would better accommodate the scale and pattern of roof ponds besides reflecting the competition's desire for more intimate, user-friendly office suites. The team evolved a design concept of radically reversing the office building's scale of the last 50 years. By using smaller units, the proposal could accommodate the modular requirements of roof ponds while achieving the urban density needed by the program.

Gradually, these concepts jelled into a building design with a mix of two and four levels of interconnected spaces occurring below a modular system of roof ponds. Our offices were able to have street address to provide the "crystal clear circulation" pattern required by the completion's program. The resulting design fit the older urban fabric to produce a design whose approach would later be identified as a case of "new urbanism."[4]

Of the 91 entries to the competition, ours was the only passive design scheme. The architectural establishment at the time found it unthinkable to abandon the mechanical conditioning of buildings. The most they imagined was to use flat-plate collectors for heating and basement rock bed thermal storage to store coolth from night ventilation for the next day. Most energy transfer was therefore by mechanically driven convection. Our scheme, in contrast, used energy transfer by radiation in the classic roof pond manner (Fig. 5.2).

The winning entry, labeled as the "Solar Slab," relied upon a very large solar collector to provide enough energy to run absorption cooling to the inhabitants located behind it or in underground offices. The "Solar Slab" approach to solar energy was used to operate mechanical systems to condition the building by the standard convection transfer with all the disadvantages and discomfort of the traditional HVAC system. Such a mechanism was the same as the interviewed people had so repeatedly complained about. In contrast, our roof pond scheme, which was calculated by Niles to provide 100% of the building's heating and cooling needs, had direct transfer of heat or coolth by radiation from pond surfaces to occupants. The ponds' structure, composed of thin steel parallelograms, took a sound diffusing shape for better acoustical quality while holding 45 tons of water for each module.

The jury consisted of State Architect Sym Van der Ryn, the head of the State Government Services who administers all state buildings, and William Caudill, an architect whose reputation was based on alternative designs

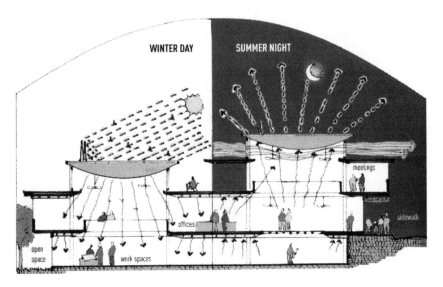

Figure 5.2 Building section with energy flow in winter day and summer night.
Source: Drawing by author.

using natural ventilation and solar control in Texas in 1950, before the
advent of air conditioning. At the time of completion he was teaching architecture at Harvard University. Caudill was impressed with the architectural
form and visual strength of the "Solar Slab" concept and quickly became the
strong voice dominating the jury.

The technical staff members of the State Architect's office, who were
younger and more radical, tried to intercede on our behalf but were soon
removed from the jury proceedings. Sim's big interest was in using this competition to push the established architects of California in the direction of
energy efficiency and social progress. A noble thought, but in terms of advan-
cing passive solar architecture, we felt the dean of the "outlaw designers"
blinked at a critical moment. California lost its chance to extend the state
of the art of roof pond buildings and we lost the chance to be in the second
phase of the competition. Later, the staff convinced the jury into giving us
an honorable mention award, which did little to help sooth our disappoint-
ment. The next state office building, the Bateson Building, designed by the
State Architect's Office, was definitely a more human, energy-efficient office
building than the solar slab and was at least as much a passive building as
a mechanical one.

The American Solar Energy Society's (ASES's) Passive Solar Conference
held in 1980 in Amherst, Massachusetts was the largest conference the
movement had been able to muster yet, with an estimated 5,000 participants.
In fact, we had reached such status that this conference even had groupies.

However, this was destined not to last. This was the last big passive energy design conference in the United States. Between 1980 and 2000 passive architecture suffered a loss of cultural favor and fervor. The reactionary politics of the Reagan era, which led to the dismantling of the Solar Energy Research Institute, the oil glut of the time and the anti-technological bias of the new trendy postmodern architecture caused projects that had been demonstrated to be efficient and effective to become passé. As the excitement evaporated, the American Solar Energy Society's active and passive solar conferences would be merged to save money.

Saving money seemed important at the time because of the drop in support from the Federal Government; however, this decision was detrimental to the culture of the passive solar movement. The inherent nature of the passive solar approach was that it required synergy between two previously relatively isolated disciplines: the designers and the thermal engineers (the conceptual and the analytical dominant sides of the effort involved). During the brief life of the passive movement there were social mechanisms that required the breaching of the silos that so plagues the industrial culture. Once removed, silo mentality was reestablished and this cultural synergy was weakened. This has hurt the solar energy movement, even to this day.

Soon the country swung back to its old wasteful ways and Hay and others who relentlessly fought for their integrated interdisciplinary research related to global environmental needs were ignored as a new energy crisis and new oil wars were spawned.[5]

It has been 40 years since Hay's roof pond system was tested and proven. During this time passive design as a movement has come and gone. There has been the rise and fall of postmodern architecture, subordinating social and technical concerns to recall and metaphor. There has been a sequence of new energy crises and middle-east oil wars. Oil prices have risen to painful highs and fallen to disruptive lows. Finally, there is recognition that the atmosphere of our planet has become the limiting condition of fossil fuel use rather than the availability of these resources.

In the continuing energy game the ante has been raised to very painful levels. We have now come to the point where climate change threatens the entire planet. Green architecture seems to have replaced postmodern architecture as trendy design but often seems equally ill defined. We have developed a defensive attitude rather than optimism about simple but highly integrated systems as we must move to zero-energy buildings. In this defensive approach we smother buildings with massive insulation, cheap photovoltaic cells, HERS ratings, green checklists, LEED certifications and multiple ever-changing prescriptive, time-consuming regulations. While such an approach is perhaps necessary for transition it is nonetheless expensive, adding to the wealth gap, and can result in architectural design by bureaucratic mandate. Complex regulations can undermine the creative potentials of design and invention. Use of energy and resources by our built environment is finally recognized as a major part of the processes driving climate disruption, so needed changes are being addressed on a larger scale. With this urgency it is important to revisit the essence of what Hay was so intensely seeking. This chapter asks: how much would it take to return to the basics? Is it still relevant to image optimization using essentially free things like solar and night radiation, and thermal mass using the cheapest material on our water planet as envisioned by Hay?

Harold Hay's legacy

To really understand Hay's legacy we need to look at his accomplishments from a cultural viewpoint. Hay as a chemist was a product of the industrial culture but as an integrationist and an inventor, he was entirely committed to cultural evolution. Underlying his inventiveness and fervor was the belief that we can grow and modify our cultural conditions and their technical responses. To Hay, the industrial era was just one step leading to the next cultural era, which was by desire and necessity an era of creativity, integration, synergy and sustainability.

Many of us involved in the passive solar movement of the 1970s were motivated by this hope. After 40 years we have to recognize there is not a quick fix in cultural evolution but a long-range effort is needed filled with obstacles and setbacks, yet there is still inevitable evolution.

It becomes easy to understand Hay's approach if we get myopic about placing ponds of water on roofs and having an entire roof consist of movable insulation. Yes, roof ponds can leak and yes, movable insulation without sophisticated industrial design development is hard to make airtight, as Steve Baer points out in his chapter in this book. The essence of Hay's work must be seen beyond the basic elements constituting his invention, and valued for the cultural shift he so early perceived. Both ponds and intermittent insulation can be considered redundant elements and could even be eliminated. However, one could still develop a Skytherm building, especially now after 40 years of technological evolution.

For the prodigious amount of thermal mass needed, we could possibly replace the water with nanotech phase-change salts like those manufactured by BASF Group. These are to be used in high-thermal-mass wallboard under the trade name "Smartboard." They can also be cast into tiles to lay on the roof or interior ceilings. Here at the San Luis Sustainability Group architecture firm, we have cast tiles containing this material and laid them in a sheet metal hammock similar to the roof ponds in our State Office Building Competition. While there have been attempts to make phase-change salts the magic bullet of thermal mass for passive solar schemes since Maria Telkes' work in the late 1940s at the Massachusetts Institute of Technology, they have always become unstable or leaked. These problems seem to have been solved now by nanotech development where the phase-change material is encapsulated in microscopic containers.

Similarly, movable insulation could be replaced with something easier to operate, longer lasting and more airtight. One possibility is something akin to Harrison's bead wall, which has operated with few problems for the last 25 years.[6] With a fresh look and without the constraints of Hay's patents, which have expired, there are many ways to evolve the Skytherm idea and remove redundancies.

Independent of how the system achieves thermal mass or how its intermittent insulation is achieved, there are four characteristics of a Skytherm building that are totally different from a standard building or a standard passive solar building. Those are:

1. Both heating and cooling are provided by the same performing elements.
2. Almost all heat transfer for heating and cooling is done by radiation. Very little is done by convection. Therefore thermal comfort is superior to most buildings.
3. The building in its flat-roof version is potentially independent of south orientation even though a solar building.
4. All rooms have the potential of equal treatment in terms of heat and coolth transfer, eliminating the bias given to south-facing rooms in direct or indirect gain passive buildings.

The essence of Hay's accomplishment is an idea very radical to an industrial culture but totally logical to a sustainable one. Such a degree of integration and reliance always made Hay's approach difficult for many people to understand, but not the technology involved. This becomes clear if we look at the characteristics of either cultures in regard to goals, conceptual tools and objectives.

The goal of our passing industrial culture is to maximize efficiency. To accomplish this, we look at parts and we simplify them, disconnect them from externalities like waste involved and make our processes as large as possible to achieve economies of scale. This results in the creation of monocultures, wealth at the expense of health and an economy of large scale. All this may sound too familiar for comfort.

Instead, the goal of the emerging sustainable culture is to maximize health. To accomplish this, sustainable-oriented designers look for holistic approaches to design, they integrate wholes and parts, consider externalities because waste can be a resource and make our processes as small as possible to reduce undesirable side effects while achieving efficiency by miniaturization. This results in the creation of polycultures, optimized wealth and health, and a synchronistic economy. Hopefully this should all sound desirable.

Miniaturization is easily understood by comparing mainframe computers of the 1950s to present cell phones. I would suggest that Hay's approach is the beginning of the miniaturization process of standard industrial-era building. Why? Because it uses on-site energies while reducing components to provide superior comfort by radiant transfer, potentially at no extra construction costs. This was Hay's original program, stated to me at the beginning of our Atascadero prototype study back in 1972.

Notes

1 The "Copper Cricket," for example, was a highly efficient solar water heater that worked like a big coffee percolator and was able to move hot water down three stories from a roof collector to storage without any pumps or moving parts.

2 Trombe walls are south-facing masonry walls glazed on the south that can serve as both passive collector and thermal storage. Bainbridge walls are similar except they used steel water tanks for thermal mass, giving them more heat storage capability. Applying a selective surface film to the south-facing thermal mass augmented the performance of these passive systems. This enhanced absorption of reduced re-radiation to the exterior.

3 Chapter 2 in this volume addresses the "design outlaw" movement as part of the 1960s and 1970s countercultural phenomena.

4 New urbanism was an architectural movement begun in the early 1980s in reaction to the problems created by suburban planning and design. It recognized the value of grid streets, alleys and mixed use of earlier cities before the dominance of the automobile.

5 Many examples abound such as the SUV craze of the 90s, the waste of electricity underlying the great California electricity crisis of 2000, etc.

6 Chapter 3 in this volume discusses Harrison's bead wall movable insulation system.

6 Determining market demand and feasibility for roof pond systems in California

William Siembieda

Harold Hay had big dreams. Part of his vision was to provide thermal heating and cooling for thousands of houses in California. In his view, the use of thermal systems would make houses more resilient to energy threats and potential rising costs, as well as lower the carbon footprint. In order to achieve this vision, Hay needed to understand the regional residential demand for thermal heating and cooling, who would build houses with such characteristics, as well as consumer preferences. He was systematic in his thinking and knew that housing is a fixed product and for the most part, not at all mobile. This presented certain problems: where housing is produced and who produces it. Unlike other manufactured goods, housing is subject to many local constraints, including land availability, local codes, finance, and consumer preference. While Hay knew a great deal about thermal dynamics and roof ponds, he knew less about the housing production system. To learn more about the regional housing system, he commissioned various studies.

This chapter examines two of these studies: flat roofs in California, New Mexico, and Arizona (2004) and housing demand in California (2002). A flat roof was Hay's preferred housing type as it allowed for simpler design, installation, and roof pond system operations. The housing demand study focused only on California, which was the most populated state in the US, and had growth potential over the next three decades. Hay wanted an estimate of future housing needs as part of a feasibility study for building a factory to mass-produce roof pond systems.

Flat roofs

In order to produce thermal roof pond systems at more than a custom-builder scale, Hay needed to establish the extent of market feasibility. The preferred roof for his system is the flat type (¼ inch sloped from the center line). In Southern California, not many flat-roof houses were being built at the time, but in Arizona and New Mexico, the opposite was true. Why was this? In 2004, a study was commissioned by Hay through the City and Regional Planning Department at California Polytechnic State University to find out its reasons.[1]

The study examined contemporary practices of builders in California, Arizona, and New Mexico who supply flat-roof units to the residential market. Custom and production builders in each state were interviewed, as well as residents of homes in New Mexico and Arizona with flat roofs. Overall, the study found that the production of flat roofs is influenced by design guidelines provided by land developers, municipalities, and market preference. At the time of the study, California had no production builders providing this product. A few custom builders in the inland California areas near Palm Springs did use this form, but in small numbers and for an upper-middle-class client group.

Flat roofs have existed in the American Southwest for more than 1,500 years.[2] The basic building system used puddle adobe walls with beams made from felled trees to form the roof frame. Brush was placed between the beams and puddle adobe covered the brush. Rains helped consolidate the roof and seal it. The Spanish colonial period (1540–1821) introduced adobe brick that replaced the puddle system and allowed for greater efficiency and larger building forms. Flat roofs have been used in Southern California since the Spanish occupation. In the late 1920s the flat-roof cottage was built in Southern California, and continued with small projects until the early 1950s. At this time, the rapid expansion after World War II created a demand for entry-level homes, some of which used tar and gravel flat roofs. But poor workmanship, leaks, and increased maintenance costs led to negative feelings about them. By the 1980s improvements in wooden truss design technology made pitched roofs an economical structural component, allowing for the elimination of interior load-bearing walls. The trusses could also be built and sourced off-site and provided developers with design flexibility (e.g., the open-floor plan with few load-bearing walls), needed to service the entry-level market. By this period, fewer California construction workers had experience with flat-roof systems, making them a more specialized product for fewer market areas.

California's contemporary flat-roof design reflects the modernist architectural form that was brought to the US from post-World War II Europe. Very good second-generation modernist design was practiced by Southern California architects, among them Gregory Ain and Rudolph Schindler. These architects, however, mostly built for the middle and upper-class market, and thus produced very few units. Ain's modernist Mar Vista project in Los Angeles, CA used flat roofs, and was designed to encourage social interaction between neighbors.[3] These units used glass panels to integrate the exterior environment with the interior space. Builder-architects such as Ned Eichler used this form in some of his San Francisco Bay Area projects, such as Foster City, where lots of light was brought in through the application of interior glass wall panels. The post-World War II expansion in California, however, was not by Europeans but by people from the Mid-West and the East Coast who did not have preferences for modernist design in a single-family home. For California, at least, migration patterns, changes in building technology, climate, and consumer preference combined to produce fewer and fewer flat-roof homes. This was not a favorable trend to expanded use of roof pond thermal systems.

Changing nature of the California regulatory and legal environment

Until the 1980s production builders in California could construct almost any style house they wanted in the marketplace. This began to change as more municipalities adopted design guidelines as tools to manage the image and form of the city. Master-planned communities began to emerge in Orange and San Diego counties. The master-planned community developers imposed their own sets of design guidelines to achieve uniform urban design between the 'villages' being built and to assure diversity and balance.[4] Irvine, Southern California's largest master-planned community (93,000 acres), begun in the late 1960s, chose a 'timeless architecture theme' using the principles of classical architecture to create a sense of continuity and ensure that communities on the Irvine Ranch would age gracefully. Because of the mild to warm climate, no houses had thermal roof applications. Flat-roof architecture was not a preferred product for these developers, as they did not fit a classical architectural approach and thus were omitted from the design guidelines. Smaller-scale builders watched what sold in the master-planned communities, and replicated much the same designs in their own projects. In addition, there was the issue of product liability in California. The law provided 10 years of consumer protection against building defects. If not properly maintained, flat roofs can, and do, leak. Several condominium projects in San Diego had poor experiences with flat roofs, leading to higher insurance rates. Consequently, for production builders this was another reason to stay away from this building type. In the high-cost custom market, however, flat roofs continue to be offered in the desert areas, as high-technology systems such as multi-layer sheet and blown foam are used. There is also a shortage of a trained labor force to install such roof systems.

In California, the places most suitable for flat-roof housing are the central and southern coastal areas, the central valley, and the inland empire (Riverside, San Bernardino, and the Coachella Valley). The builder behavior in each of these areas takes on different forms. Large firms, however, such as Pulte and Centex (no longer in business), did build flat-roof products in Arizona and New Mexico, but not in California. Evidently, market preferences do play a part, as we learn in the next section.

One developer, in the Coachella Valley, built a 92-unit flat-roof project with a southwestern theme in 2000. The project sold out on schedule, and was well received. The firm, however, will not continue this building type because of higher building costs and construction defect liability and insurance costs. From a regulatory viewpoint, one technical advantage was that it is easier to meet maximum allowable height restrictions for local codes using the flat-roof design.

Arizona and New Mexico

The American Southwest has a generally dry climate and high temperature in the desert areas. It is also influenced by the Spanish and Mexican architectural forms. Interviews with 12 builders were conducted in 2003.[5] All the builders, whether production or custom, had experience with flat-roof design. More than a third of them built more than 50% of the homes with flat roofs. The main factors for flat-roof production were: market demand, cost efficiency, familiarity with building systems, and developer restrictions on lots purchased for building. These builders constructed for all market segments and their work responded to the 'style' of the subdivisions. In the Civano master-planned community, near Tucson, AZ, that began building in 1999, design guidelines promote the southwestern identity which features flat roofs and a range of environmental control systems in the design including active solar. Thermal mass was used only in the walls. Cooling towers were incorporated, at times, for heat reduction. In this community, advanced at the time, thermal roof ponds were not included. Andres Duany, a designer from Civano, notes: "We designed buildings with flat roofs and stucco, influenced in part by Santa Fe architecture, but also because these elements are best suited for this climate."[6]

In New Mexico, the Tierra Contenta project operated by the Housing Trust, a Santa Fe non-profit corporation, promoted flat roofs. Some builders included energy-conscious design in their products with passive solar, site orientation, and photovoltaic being featured. These vary according to the price of the house. What is built constitutes a constellation of many factors. In the Civano, Arizona development, for example, passive solar standards are part of the city requirements, while in other cities, building permit fees are lowered for projects that include passive solar. The biggest issue for flat roofs in the southwest is maintaining them. Commercial buildings have scheduled maintenance, whereas residential buildings do not. The variation in residential maintenance is the factor that effects leakage the most. Flat roofs experience less leakage and maintenance problems in low-precipitation zones of the southwest, but are less suited to mountainous or snowy zones.

A consumer survey of house owners, in Tucson, Arizona and Albuquerque, New Mexico, was done in 2003 to determine their preferences and issues with flat roofs.[7] Most people interviewed (N=11) liked flat-roof houses and would buy or rent one again. They found the design aesthetically pleasing. Most respondents chose the homes for the exterior style. The style, referred to as 'Santa Fe,' is part of the home attraction. Maintenance is an issue for respondents, which explains why 82% knew about flat-roof construction and composition. Overall, 92% said they would purchase or rent a flat-roof home again. From the 1980s the 'southwestern and pueblo revival' styles were further popularized by tract and custom builders. Figure 6.1 depicts

Figure 6.1 Southwestern house in Corrales, New Mexico, 1997.
Source: Photo: Leslie Siembieda.

a New Mexico home equipped with trombe passive solar walls and a roof-active solar water heating system. This trend was strongly reflected in 2004's Santa Fe Home Builders publication 'Hacienda – A Parade of Homes,' which featured 33 projects, 31 of them with flat-roof designs.

What was apparent in the study was the regional diversity. Since the 1960s, California has been moving away from flat-roof designs for residential projects, while Arizona and New Mexico continue to embrace this design in their regional contexts. The impact of regional differences was found in the size of the markets, with California being far bigger than Arizona and New Mexico combined.[8] Certainly to commercialize Hay's roof pond system, the market should have included California.

Estimating housing demand in California

Hay recognized that California was the market to target for a thermal roof pond system. He wanted to build a factory in Southern California for production. The size of the factory would depend on the size of the new housing market over a 25-year period. Developing projections for a particular product demand has its challenges. Such projections influenced obtaining funding from investors to build the factory. Having worked in the wood products industry early in his career, Hay was aware of the need for a feasibility study to estimate potential demand. Understanding that the highest demand would occur in the most populated and sunny areas, only a selected part of California was used for the study. The Tehachapi mountain range separates Southern from Northern California; the Central Valley, east of the coastal zone, was chosen as a northern boundary line for projecting the housing demand.[9] The counties in the projection area are those whose degree days and precipitation characteristics would benefit most from the application of a roof pond system to control thermal conditions. Two Central Valley counties, Fresno and Kern, were added as their degree days were high enough for inclusion and both were areas for future increased population expansion.

Housing demand in the US, and in California, is typically cyclical. There are periods of expansion and contraction, with peaks and valleys. No one really knows how high the peaks or how deep the valleys will be until they happen. Since 1973, California has experienced five cycles ranging from three to nine years. The cycles were becoming longer. The cycle length is a function of household formation, job expansion, mortgage interest rates, zoning, and land availability. What happened in the past, therefore, provides only partial information on what will occur in the future. The overall study design for Hay's objective was to create an 'opportunity model' that would provide both locational and quantitative projections. Understanding that any projection beyond a 10-year period is subject to high variation, the projection estimates were made for three levels: optimistic, moderate, and conservative.

A mix of urban expansion theories established some competing views. It began with a review of California housing cycles from 1970–2000. Data acquired from the Construction Industries Research Board was used to inform the investigation. Both housing cycle and demographic theories were implemented as they provided competing views of the future. Housing cycle theory (based on starts) established the periodicity: the time between a trough and a peak (in months or years), as well as the slope which indicates how gradual or rapid decline or expansion could occur. Demographic theory provided the rate of household formation, and if this is strong, then the demand can outstrip the supply. Using the annual rates of housing starts against the household formations for a decade allowed us to visualize a picture of the housing market dynamics.

Housing component theory was used to account for the stock withdrawals: demolitions and replacement of substandard units. The higher the stock withdrawals, the more replacement units will be needed. Supply theory looks at the system capacity to produce units, using the production rates of the 1990s. This is particularly important in California which has a strong regulatory system of land use and environmental laws, making supply subject to the time required to obtain subdivision and housing permits prior to construction. These are considered lags in the system that slow down supply response to demand.

Data assembly

Initially, a review was conducted that found no public or private organization published a 2000–2015 housing projection based on more than a single theory. For example, some organizations published 10-year projections without constraint considerations. This is likely to overestimate actual production. In this study, two main data sets and three secondary sets were used. The first set is composed of the 2000–2010 and the 2000–2025 projections by the regional metropolitan planning organizations (or councils of government, COG) south of Tehachapi region (SOT). The second major set of data were the building permits of all municipalities from 1990–2001.[10] The minor data sets consulted were from the California Housing and Community Development Departments, the US Department of Housing and Urban Development's US Housing Market Conditions, and the University of Southern California Futures Project.[11]

Three basic projections were completed: optimistic, moderate, and conservative. The optimistic projections are those of the SOT-COGs.[12] The moderate projection uses one standard deviation above the mean, calculated on the previous period approach. The conservative projection uses the previous period's (1990–2001) mean when the COG projections exceed one standard deviation above it; otherwise the COG projection is accepted.

The projections yielded dramatic variation, with nearly a million units' difference between the optimistic and the conservative (Table 6.1).[13] Even at a conservative level, there was a large enough market, so production of even a small share (<10%) would likely have provided commercial feasibility for the Hay system.

Fitting the models into a pragmatic approach

Prudent projections of how many houses could actually be built over a 25-year period is an exercise in pragmatism. While population and job growth are demand indicators, they are not perfect substitutes for actual housing supply. Since Hay was interested in what actually might be built, this study

Table 6.1 Projection summary 2000–2025 south of Tehachapi Group of counties

	Optimistic	*Moderate*	*Conservative*
Total Units	2,568,917	2,296,551	1,635,739
Annual Average	102,757	91,862	65,430

Source: Siembieda, Bergman, and Firestine, 2002

used a pragmatic decision model in preparing the projections. The ones from the SOT-COGs were done in five-year periods. These were then annualized. Against these projections, the actual annual construction housing data from the previous period provided an annual figure for the prior five years. This offered a historical mean (average). If the SOT-COG-forecasted figure was within one standard deviation of the historical mean, the forecast was accepted for the jurisdiction. For example, if the City of Vista, CA had 30,000 total units in 2000 and forecasted 35,000 units by 2005, it was forecasting a sustained 1,000 units increment per year, for five years. If the CIRB data indicated that the City of Vista had a mean of 700 total units a year for the past decade, using the one standard deviation method, we accepted that the forecasts were within one standard deviation of the mean, in this case 350 units. Consequently, the local COG projection would be used. If the local COG figure exceeded one standard deviation, it was rejected, and the historical mean would be used for the jurisdiction. This approach does not take into account where the city is in the actual housing cycle; that is on the upslope or at the trough. But given that the factory Hay wanted to build would be operating over the long term, the cycle problems would be considered part of general business adjustments to production, meaning the factory needed to have flexibility to expand and contract quickly.

Celebrating the model

While the housing projection study did not lead to building a roof pond factory in Southern California, the question can be asked: did the method yield reliable projections? The method can be tested by using the actual historical data on housing starts (single and multiple units), built in 2013 and 2016 for the three counties: Los Angeles, Riverside, and Orange. The moderate and conservative projections made at the time of the study (2004) do fit the 2013 and 2016 actuals. The optimistic projections, however, are low. This was due to California emerging from the US financial crisis of 2008. Such national events are beyond the scope of any regional housing projection model. Actually, optimistic projections must assume a consistent level of market stability, which in the US is not supported by historical events. The actual study was advising Hay to use conservative projections, as these are the most stable in terms of modeling approaches.

Locational methodology

This section presents the locational factors that would constrain development as well as identify opportunities. This was done alongside the projection models to identify specific growth location, and inform Hay on where a factory site might be best selected. The model locates areas of California that are the most conductive to using roof ponds as a means of passive heating and cooling. The location aspects consist of constructing a Geographic

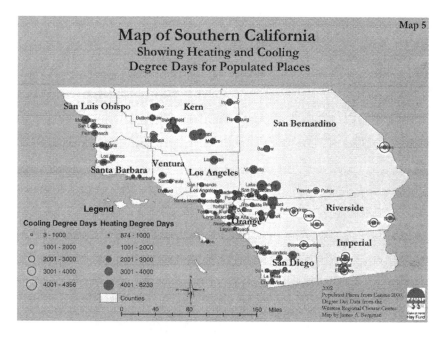

Figure 6.2 Heating and cooling day map.
Source: Siembieda, Bergman, and Firestine, 2002.

Information System (GIS) that includes data about the physical features of the state and links the features with the climate and production data. This study used altitude, heating, and cooling degree days, precipitation data, and climate zones.[14] A base map of all the state's settlements was initially created. This included 548 cities, the 58 counties. Then, constraints maps based on elevation and populated areas were made to further the study. The heating and cooling day maps allowed for sub-regional identification that could be used for marketing purposes (Fig. 6.2).

Discussion

Hay's vision was to use the flat-roof housing form for roof pond systems to be manufactured in Southern California. The California market would provide the test-of-concept needed to propel the system nationally. At the time, there was only a nascent understanding of climate change based on renewable energy and climate adaptation needs. Hay was at least 20 years ahead of his time in that roof pond applications are energy savers, and contribute to reducing greenhouse gas emissions. In 2006, California passed AB 32, the Global Warming Solutions Act, that established the state's interest in energy reduction and greenhouse gas reduction.[15] In 2018, for example, California

Cap and Trade funding assisting vulnerable community efforts would have favored roof pond system installations. This funding addressed special needs through support for the Low-Income Weatherization Program.

Even though the projections established that there could be a market in Southern California for a roof pond application, the expansion of solar products (electric and for water heating) dominated consumer and builder interest in energy-related options. The fact that there was only one test house built in the 1970s, and that the building community had little interest in applying the product and sorting out the construction liability, were barriers to entry for Hay. In practical terms the costs of electric and gas have decreased the economic savings roof pond systems might have afforded the user. The costs to build a factory, market a new product, and gain market share were too great to overcome. Hay's big dream could not be realized given changes in technology, and the absence of supporters in the building community.

Notes

1 William Siembieda and Corinne Rosenblum, *Flat Roof Housing in California and the American Southwest. Opportunities for Expanded Use* (San Luis Obispo, CA: California Polytechnic State University: Evelyn and Harold Hay Fund, 2004).

2 Bainbridge Bunting, *Early Architecture of New Mexico* (Albuquerque, NM: University of New Mexico Press. 1976).

3 Mar Vista Tract, accessed December 17, 2017, www.marvistatract.org/history.html.

4 William Siembieda and Jerry Sturmer, "Master Planned Communities: Design and Planning Makes an Enduring Difference," *Real Estate Review* 41, no. 1 (2012): 75–90.

5 The field interviews in New Mexico were conducted by Shelley Maynard. The Arizona field interviews were conducted by Rich Michal. All interviews were under the direction of William Siembieda who wrote the interview instrument.

6 Simmons B. Buntin, "Unsprawl Case Study: Community of Civano, Arizona," accessed December, 17, 2017, www.terrain.org/unsprawl/5.

7 The consumer interviews in New Mexico were conducted by Shelley Maynard, and the Arizona interviews by Rich Michal.

8 The 2010 US Census reports that California had 13,680,081 housing units while Arizona has 2,844,526, and New Mexico had 901,386.

9 These mountains are located southeast of Bakersfield and the Central Valley, and west of Mojave and the Antelope Valley. The Tejon Pass runs through them, along what is called the Grapevine route connecting Kern County to Los Angeles County.

10 Construction Industry Research Board, *Residential Permits by City and County Data File 1990–2001* (Burbank, CA: 2001).

11 California Department of Housing and Community Development, Housing Policy Development Division, *Raising the Roof: California Housing Development Projections and Constraints, 1997–2020* (Sacramento, CA: 2000).

12 These have a bias, in that the organizations compete for transportation funding and higher growth brings more funding. So, projections of housing expansion are higher throughout the region.

13 William Siembieda, James A. Bergman, and Andrew Firestone, *Housing Production South of the Tehachapi Range: A 2000–2025 Projection* (San Luis Obispo, CA: California Polytechnic State University: Evelyn and Harold Hay Fund, 2002).

14 A degree day compares the outside temperature to a standard 65 degrees Fahrenheit (F); the more extreme the temperature, the higher the degree day number. Thus, degree-day measurement can be used to describe the effect of outdoor temperature on the amount of energy needed for space heating or cooling.

15 Four California Climate Change Assessments have been produced (2006, 2009, 2012, and 2017 – Draft). Each of these focused in more detail on built environment components of energy conservation and greenhouse gas reduction. The roof pond system could have been part of the overall solution, if adopted on a regional basis.

Part II
Active repercussions

7 Creating the context for a solar future

Two activists, two buildings

Robert Peña

Two giants of the modern solar energy movement, both recognized by the American Solar Energy Society with the Charles Greeley Abbot Award for significant contributions to the field of solar energy, are probably better known for the contributions they made in other parts of their lives.[1] A farm boy and inventor, Harold Hay was still in college when he developed the formula for a wood preservative that was later developed into what became the standard treatment for telephone poles and railroad ties used world-wide ever since. Denis Hayes was a 25-year-old college student when he organized the first Earth Day in 1970, a "national teach-in on the environment" that launched the modern environmental movement and is now the largest annual secular holiday in the world.[2]

Two very different men born 35 years apart and raised on opposite sides of Washington's Cascade Mountains, Hay and Hayes shared a mission to steer society toward a more equitable and sustainable future. They understood that in most places it's possible to make affordable buildings that deliver services of heating, cooling, ventilation and lighting using only site-available resources. They also knew that to get people to think seriously about these kinds of buildings the concept needed to be demonstrated. By building and operating a fully functional, comfortable and beautiful building, powered only by the sun and other site resources, the context is created for a different kind of building with a very different relationship to both energy and the environment.

The ideas and activism of Hay and Hayes have inspired generations of designers, activists and organizers. And while the elegant Skytherm concept awaits its moment in the sun, the Bullitt Center's moment is here and its influence is emerging in a new generation of green, climate-responsive solar buildings worldwide.

Two activists

Both men grew up in the State of Washington; Hay in Spokane on the dry golden east side of the Cascades, and Hayes on the wet green west side of the mountains along the Columbia River in the small paper mill town of Camas.

Hay came of age during the Great Depression and learned early in life the value of thrift and compassion. He experienced the desperate poverty of the early 1920s which planted in him a deep commitment to helping those in need. He was a practical, 'hands-on' problem solver with the mind of a scientist and the 'can-do' competence of a farmer. If there was a problem to solve he dug in and got to work on it, whether it was cleaning up political corruption as a young community organizer and political activist in St. Louis in the 1930s, or later in his career, building inexpensive climate-responsive houses in India.[3]

Hayes came of age in the 1960s under a very different set of social, political and economic circumstances. His father worked in the local paper mill where Hayes saw first-hand the disregard in the paper industry for both worker protections and environmental health. There was no pollution control of any kind. Twenty-four hours a day, 365 days a year, the mill filled the sky for 25 miles downwind with sulfur dioxide and hydrogen sulfide. The stench was what people from Portland thought of Camas. The result was both acid precipitation that corroded roofs and air pollution that harmed lungs. Hayes began connecting these local threats to people and the environment with larger patterns of threats to human health and the environment emerging around the world (Fig. 7.1).

The public was also beginning to make these connections. In 1962 Rachel Carson published *Silent Spring*, alerting the world to the consequences of widespread pesticide use.[4] In 1968, American biologist Paul Ehrlich published *The Population Bomb*, which warned of mass starvation and social upheaval unless immediate action was taken to limit population growth.[5] Concurrently, the Vietnam War was in full swing and the country was vigorously debating its role as the world's superpower. Antiwar teach-ins took place at 120 campuses across the country aimed at practical, participatory and action-oriented outcomes.[6] Across the country people were voicing concerns about the disconnect between the economic means by which progress is measured and the health of the biosphere that is the source of our health and well-being.

This was the context for the first Earth Day, a global teach-in on the biosphere. Hayes, who was a student at Harvard University, was recruited by Senator Gaylord Nelson to be the national coordinator. The first Earth Day events took place on April 22, 1970, in thousands of colleges and universities, primary and secondary schools, in hundreds of cities across the country. Hayes said, "it brought twenty million Americans out into the spring sunshine for peaceful demonstrations in favor of environmental reform." They participated in rallies, teach-ins and clean-up efforts to demonstrate their commitment to environmental action and press for legislation to secure the health of our land, air and water. Earth Day set the stage for the most significant environmental protection laws ever enacted.[7]

Hayes and other activists in the environmental movement applied scientific evidence to make their arguments for the fundamental changes needed in modern society's relationship to the environment. They used an approach

Figure 7.1 Denis Hayes.
Source: Photo courtesy of Denis Hayes.

for predicting the trajectory of an environmental trend that he called the "self-undoing hypothesis," a kind of mirror image of the 'self-fulfilling prophecy.'[8] The idea was to look back at how things had evolved in recent times then project these out 10, 20 or 30 years into the future. Charting the exponentially rising trend lines of population and energy growth, air and water pollution, and most importantly, atmospheric CO_2, the trajectory of all these metrics provided compelling evidence that our industrial society needed to change course, and fast. Earth Day and the discussions that followed, along with kids in gas masks making their voices heard in places all around the country, led directly to the enactment of the Clean

Air Act in 1970, and within five years to the Clean Water Act, the Marine Mammal Protection Act, the Environmental Education Act, the Superfund and the Environmental Protection Agency.

Twenty years earlier, Hay had moved to Sweden and was working as a chemist, developing methods to make more efficient use of waste wood for fiber board. It was satisfying work that aligned with his values. He was taking a waste product and turning it into useful material for building afford-able houses and furniture, unknowingly setting the stage for mass-produced flat-pack furniture. While there, he heard President Truman deliver his 1949 inaugural address known as the 'Four Point Speech.' In this speech, Truman announced his 'Point Four' program, a "bold new program for making the benefits of our scientific advances and industrial progress available for the improvement and growth of underdeveloped nations."[9] Hay had been pro-posing similar initiatives to both the US Embassy in Sweden and at the State Department in Washington, DC, so he knew that he had to be part of it and returned to the United States to join the program. Because of his interdiscip-linary background as an engineer and as a materials scientist, he was hired by the Housing and Home Finance Agency who sent him to India as an International Building Materials Advisor.[10]

When Hay arrived in India his first assignment was to design a small house that people with limited means could build themselves. He had never built a house before but that didn't slow him down. As the dauntless sci-entist and hands-on problem solver he was, he started by researching the problem and testing solutions. The primary limitation was the sheer poverty of the people he was designing for. They had no money and only the most rudimentary working tools. Always looking for the simplest and most ele-gant solution to any problem, he tested different designs and arrived at his first prototype: a mud-walled, bamboo and thatched-roof house. The house was very modest, just one room plus a kitchen with a stove made from a 10-quart bucket propped up on a couple of bricks with a simple little cowshed on the side. The basic house cost about $80. But in four incremental stages, the basic dwelling could be upgraded until it was a very respectable home which cost about $500.

While the first house got a lot of positive attention in India and in British journals, Hay wasn't satisfied because the house wasn't very comfortable on sunny days. It worked well on the typically cool nights of the region, retaining the heat of the day in its mud walls for warmth at night. But during the day it was uncomfortably warm due to the exposed roof which heated in the sunshine, radiating this heat into the space. This was fine in the winter but not so fine in the summer.

He realized that the solution was a timeless one: to design with the cli-mate and to use the large day-to-night temperature swings to best advan-tage. And this got him thinking about nocturnal radiation: in a climate with clear dry air, the effect of radiation loss to the night sky is strong enough to freeze water, even when the air temperatures are above freezing. This principle has been used in the Middle East for centuries to make ice at night in the desert.

Hay believed that the first step in addressing a complex problem is to confine it to its simplest terms. In this case, the problem was to design comfort into an extremely low-cost house in an arid climate with large diurnal temperature swings. The basic goals were to protect the building's living area from solar heat during the day and open it up at night to radiate heat to the night sky. Viewed in these simple terms, the solution was clear: move dry panels of insulation back and forth from day to night to control the heat and thermal environment of the house. Hay called this the "drytherm" principle. So what Hay initially thought of as a failure turned out to be his first building's greatest success: a revelation about nocturnal radiation and movable insulation which would ultimately become his life's work.

On the heels of Earth Day and the transformative environmental legislation that followed came the oil embargo of 1973–74 by the Organization of Arab Petroleum Exporting Countries, a response to US support of Israel during the Yom Kippur War. This embargo exposed our dependence on imported oil and our vulnerability to disruptions from sources outside of our control. Gasoline availability was disrupted and prices nearly doubled in some parts of the country. For a nation that had come to expect cheap and plentiful energy as our birthright, the oil shock of 1973–74 was a major wake-up call. It got Americans thinking about smaller cars and alternative sources of energy, and it opened the political landscape to an outsider from Plains, Georgia, who spoke of the imperative to transform the nation's energy economy from one dependent on fossil fuels to one powered by renewable energy.

Shortly after his election in 1976, President Jimmy Carter established two new cabinet-level departments, the Department of Education and the Department of Energy. He also established a national energy policy that included conservation, price controls and technology development. In 1977, President Carter launched the Solar Energy Research Institute (SERI) to realize these policies, and he appointed Denis Hayes to be its director. SERI was established as the nation's primary laboratory for renewable energy and energy efficiency research and development. It also sought to develop and promote knowledge about existing technologies like passive solar energy for heating buildings. President Carter articulated a plan for improving energy efficiency in our cars, homes and industries, and a vision to achieve the goal of getting 20% of the nation's energy from renewable sources by the year 2000. The concept for this 20-year plan was drawn from Hayes' 1977 book, *Rays of Hope: The Transition to a Post-Petroleum World.*[11] The detailed policies to achieve this goal were contained in a huge study produced by SERI with assistance from other national laboratories and several universities.[12] President Carter announced this ambitious plan just a few months before losing the presidential election to Ronald Reagan in 1980.

Reagan did not share these goals, nor did he embrace the idea of a renewable-energy future. In a demonstration of the new administration's return to the past, he removed the solar panels that had been installed on the White House roof, and he virtually dismantled SERI. When Reagan was elected, SERI had an operating budget of $140 million, devoted exclusively to renewable energy. It was a hotbed of innovation, spending more money on renewable-energy research and obtaining more patents than the rest of the world altogether. But just six months after taking office, the Reagan Administration reduced SERI's budget by $110 million to $30 million. One-third of the staff was fired, as were all of the contractors. Two of these fired contractors went on to win Nobel Prizes.[13]

Two buildings

Hay's first mud buildings in India led to the idea of movable insulation, an elegantly simple solution akin to using a blanket – all you needed to do is change the position of the insulation panels. In fact, it may have seemed too simple for the people he was designing for. While the foreign press lauded the idea, it was not accepted locally. What he came to understand was that in developing countries, people did not want to use a simple idea if it was thought to be only good enough for them and not for people in developed countries. He realized that for this concept to take root in India he needed to change the context. For this technology to be embraced in the developing world, it would first need to be accepted and used in the United States, Britain or France.[14]

Creating a context where solar buildings are the accepted norm rather than the exception was a central goal for the creation of the Bullitt Center. After leaving SERI in 1981, Hayes went back to school and completed a law degree at Stanford Law School, taught in the Stanford School of Engineering and worked as a litigator in the Bay Area.[15] Since 1992, Hayes has been the president and CEO of the Bullitt Foundation, a Seattle non-profit whose mission is a "future that safeguards the vitality of natural ecosystems while accommodating a sustainable human population in healthy, vibrant, equitable, and prosperous communities."[16] The Bullitt Center, a 50,000-square-foot commercial office building Seattle, is one manifestation of this vision (Fig. 7.2).

Hay's idea for a climate-responsive solar house employing movable insulation and thermal mass to achieve thermal comfort without burning fossil fuels developed through a series of experimental efforts over the 20 years following the first houses he built in India. These experiments reached their most resolved and celebrated form in the Atascadero house, completed in 1973. The Atascadero house, like the Bullitt Center, encapsulated the values of its creator and ethos of the solar movement of its time. It was designed around an elegantly simple concept distilled to the fewest parts necessary to make it work. It eschewed expensive technology with a modernist 'less-is-more' attitude. In its years as an inhabited, single-family residence, it

Figure 7.2 Bullitt Center.
Source: Photograph courtesy of Nic Lehoux.

performed brilliantly, requiring virtually no purchased energy for heating or cooling.[17]

The Atascadero house and the Bullitt Center, though radically different in scale, climate and context, are both intimately connected to and adapted for their climate, place and purpose. In the summer, they both take advantage of cool nights to flush the heat stored in their floors and walls to ready themselves for cool comfort on warm afternoons. In cold weather, they both have tight, well-insulated building envelopes to keep the heat in and cold out. For additional warmth in the winter, the Atascadero house uses solar heat stored in the roof pond, water in a sealed bag used as a thermal "battery" to store and discharge heat. The Bullitt Center also uses stored heat, but its source is the warmth in the earth beneath the building, accessed with the help of ground-source heat pumps. They both implement architectural or 'passive' strategies to deliver services of heating, cooling, illumination and fresh air with minimal mechanical means. It is only after these architectural strategies can no longer provide the needed environmental services that integrated mechanical systems kick in.

The Bullitt Center constitutes a paradigm shift in outlook from the 20th-century idea of buildings as 'machines for living' to the idea of buildings as 'living systems': from buildings that are utterly dependent on energy-intensive machinery to deliver environmental services, to climate-responsive buildings designed as integrated architectural systems powered by renewable energy. A 'living building' is a system of systems, both architectural and mechanical, that work together to deliver thermal comfort, daylight and fresh air. Just as the pores in our skin help regulate temperature, if it's too warm or the air is too stuffy indoors, the windows open for fresh, cool air. If it's too cold, the windows stay shut and a heat recovery ventilator (HRV) delivers fresh air from outside, tempered by the warm exhaust air leaving the building. And like the iris of an eye, exterior louvered blinds deploy and adjust to regulate direct sunlight, scatter daylight into the building and reduce the need for cooling.

Harold Hay the scientist demanded evidence, and for a building the proof is in its performance. He would approve of the ongoing work to document the Bullitt Center's operation and continually improve its performance. During its first three years in operation, the Bullitt Center generated 60% more energy with the PV panels on its roof than it used; it can supply users with all the water needed for drinking, showers and cleaning with the rainwater it captures on the roof; it composts on-site the waste from its toilets and urinals and returns used water from sinks and showers to the environment in an undiminished state; and it is built from materials that do no harm to people or the planet. It is a building whose relationship to the hydrosphere is about the same as the Douglas fir forest that occupied this site 150 years ago.

The Atascadero House has been both the definitive source of performance data on roof-pond technology and a source of inspiration for a generation of educators and passive solar advocates. It is a brilliant concept that represents a design ethos that has changed our approach to making high-performance buildings. And while it hasn't changed the world, its inspiration and the spirit of Hay's ideas may yet be championed and developed in new ways in the future.

When the Bullitt Center was dedicated, Hayes said that if "the Bullitt Center is still the greenest building in the world five years from now, it will have been a waste. The whole purpose is to be an agent of change."[18] Now nearly five years after its completion, it may still be the 'greenest' building of its scale and kind, but there is evidence of its influence. There are at least two 'living buildings' of similar scale under development and a number of other large, institutional buildings in the US that are considering Living Building™ certification. The Edge in Amsterdam, an even larger commercial office building that employs many of the same design strategies as the Bullitt Center along with a host of other new technologies, has branded itself as the "world's greenest building," largely because of its energy and water efficiency. Design and development teams from all of these projects have visited the Bullitt Center, along with delegations from around the world. Since its opening in 2013, an estimated 205,000 visitors have toured the building. While still mostly anecdotal, evidence of its influence is emerging in a new generation of high-performance buildings here in Seattle and across the country.

Both pioneering solar advocates understood the importance of evidence; of proving an idea by building it and examining its performance. Once something is demonstrated, people start to think about it more seriously. Both men understood that for their ideas about high-performance buildings to be accepted, they had to create the context and a new norm for this new kind of building. And both buildings demonstrate a different and more balanced relationship with technology than our fossil-fueled, mechanically dependent buildings of the 20th century. Both buildings re-orient the relationship between buildings and the environment, demonstrating that comfort, convenience, beauty and sustainability are compatible goals for a building.

These two buildings helped create a new context, a new operational norm for buildings and a new threshold for performance expectations. The Bullitt Center created a new regulatory context that makes it easier to create a building that collects its own water, purifies and returns wastewater to the environment, composts its toilet waste on-site, and is paid by the local utility for its performance. Closing these resource loops at the scale of a building is an important demonstration, but not necessarily an environmental imperative in Seattle where these services are responsibly supplied by the City. But it does invite this question: what is the appropriate scale for a power plant, water treatment plant and wastewater treatment facility? Is it the scale of a building, a neighborhood, a city or a region? The answer depends on context. For cities in developing countries where power is often unreliable, sanitation unavailable and water quality questionable, it provides a model for delivering these services at the scale of a building. Hay believed that buy-in from wealthy western nations would help win acceptance for his ideas in the developing world. Accepted and emulated here, the Bullitt Center is a model for cities in the developing world for leaping past 20th-century technology and infrastructure to a different and more sustainable approach for making buildings in the 21st century.

Notes

1 American Solar Energy Society, awards-fellows: Charles Greely Abbot Award, accessed July 7, 2017, www.ases.org/about/awards-fellows/charles-greeley-abbot-award.
2 Earth Day Network, The History of Earth Day, accessed January 15, 2018, www.earthday.org/about/the-history-of-earth-day.
3 Mother Earth News Editors (September/October 1976), "Plowboy Interview: Harold R. Hay Talks about Solar Energy," interview by Mother Earth News, accessed May 5, 2017, www.motherearthnews.com/nature-and-environment/harold-r-hay-zmaz76soztak.
4 Rachel Carson, *Silent Spring* (Boston, MA: Houghton Mifflin Company, 1962).
5 Paul R. Ehrlich, *The Population Bomb* (New York: Sierra Club/Ballantine Books, 1968).

6 Charles DeBenedetti and Charles Chatfield (assisting), *An American Ordeal: The Antiwar Movement of the Vietnam Era* (1st ed.) (Syracuse, NY: Syracuse University Press, 1990).

7 Denis Hayes and Jason McLennon, "The Next 50 at Seattle Center: Reflections on the 50th Anniversary of the Seattle Space Needle," a conversation with Denis Hayes and Jason McLennon, May 10, 2012.

8 Ibid.

9 Harry S. Truman, "1949 Inaugural Address," text of the speech in *Department of State Bulletin* (January 30, 1949): 123.

10 Mother Earth News Editors (September/October 1976), "Plowboy Interview."

11 Denis Hayes, *Rays of Hope: The Transition to a Post-Petroleum World* (New York: W.W. Norton & Company, 1977).

12 SERI, *A New Prosperity: The SERI Solar-Conservation Study* (Brick House Publishing, 1981).

13 Hayes and McLennon, "The Next 50 at Seattle Center," 2012.

14 Mother Earth News Editors, "Plowboy Interview."

15 Beverly Beyette, "Environmentalists Weigh Achievements, Challenges" (*Los Angeles Times*, May 30, 1985), accessed May 5, 2017, http://articles.latimes.com/1985-05-30/news/vw-5260_1_environmental-movement.

16 Bullitt Foundation Mission, accessed January 13, 2018, www.bullitt.org/about/mission.

17 Elizabeth Douglas, "A Pioneer Refuses to Fade Away: His Passion for Solar Still Burns" (*Los Angeles Times*, November 10, 2007), accessed June 6, 2017, http://articles.latimes.com/2007/nov/10/business/fi-haroldhay10.

18 Denis Hayes, address at the Dedication of the Bullitt Center, April 22, 2013.

8   Shade, mass and water
Activism by degrees

John S. Reynolds

Harold Hay was never mentioned during my architectural education. Neither was passive design. The University of Illinois in the late 1950s catered to "starchitecture" in design studios, and the history of modern architecture class favored buildings rather than systems. At MIT in the mid-1960s, the earlier passive pioneers such as Maria Telkes had faded from memory, and the only course concerned with environmental control systems was Robert Newman's excellent acoustics seminar.

So, I began my teaching career at the University of Oregon in 1967 with scant preparation for the less mechanical aspects of environmental control systems (ECS). I quickly found that the rudiments of my undergraduate ECS classes – equation memorization and their numerical results – were not what motivated students to make their design decisions. They were more interested in "why" than "how to."

Thanks to the American Solar Energy Society (ASES), I met other educators interested in motivating design students toward a renewable energy future. Pioneers such as Harold Hay came to light. His experiments with the Skytherm system blended my interest in three elements of passive architecture: shade, water and mass. Better yet, Skytherm expected its users to be actively involved in operation. And as I witnessed at many fiery ASES meetings, Hay was himself an outspoken solar activist. He was an inspiration.

Shade

The sun's impact on buildings is central to passive design. In 1968 I began a series of exterior photos of six Eugene, Oregon buildings with east, south and west facades. I photographed them at three times a day, at all four solstice/equinox days. Remembering exactly the shooting position three months earlier was one challenge; finding direct sunlight around the winter solstice was another in the cloudy winter Pacific Northwest.

The resulting series revealed several unanticipated benefits accompanying both seasonal and daily change: the sky and daylight color shifts, the seasonal impact of deciduous vegetation, occupant behavior with

Figure 8.1 South-facing facades near solar noon in Eugene, Oregon. (Left) On the
autumnal equinox, (Right) On the vernal equinox.

Source: Photographs by author.

opening/closing windows and people's degree of clothing. An emphasis on
change is refreshing and challenging. It reminds us that while architects
give birth to building designs, it is the inhabitants who live with them.
Methodically documenting simple situations added much to notions of
aesthetic and social richness, and sparked an interest in deciduous shading
(Fig. 8.1).

Deciduous vegetation's season lags that of the sun. The longest day of
the year – summer solstice – is rarely the hottest, so the deciduous tree or
vine has not yet reached its point of most-dense shade. The truly hot days
of July and August are the times of maximum leaf size, darkest color and
maximum thickness. The autumnal equinox marks the beginning of fall, but
the deciduous plant retains its leaves because of the still-warm weather. As
the days grow shorter and cooler, the leaves lighten in color and eventually
fall. This exposes a building's windows to the warming rays of the sun. The
shortest day of the year – winter solstice – is rarely the coldest, and by now
the deciduous plant is completely bare. Maximum solar access for windows
therefore results. The vernal equinox marks the beginning of spring, but the
deciduous plant stays bare, allowing solar access through these continuing

cool days. As the days become longer and hotter, buds grow into leaves and provide increasing shade.

Designers who provide fixed-geometry shading devices for windows face a spring/fall dilemma. A south-facing window can be easily provided with an overhang that shades the entire window on June 21, and no shading on December 21. But that will result in half-shade on both the spring and fall equinox. This is too much sun in September, and not enough sun in March. The deciduous vine or tree instead works better and performs as a living awning.

Mass

In the late 1970s the Carter administration supported the development of solar energy. During this time of peaking interest, an eccentric solar house using water-heating collectors turned up in cloudy Coos Bay, Oregon, obtaining most of its winter heat from the sun. A massive storage tank was built first, then the house over it.[1] This house's technical and social aspects were appealing; its aesthetics were not. Sure, solar architecture could be practical, but what about its aesthetics?

To answer that question, Edward Mazria was recruited to join our faculty for two years. He wrote much of his *Passive Solar Energy Book* while in residence in Eugene.[2] The extensive windows of the passive solar approach appealed far more than the large and awkward collectors of active solar, and design students responded with enthusiasm. We revisited the book *Your Solar House: A Book of Practical Homes for All Parts of the Country* edited in 1947 by Maron J. Simon, published by Simon and Schuster and sponsored by glass maker Libbey Owens Ford. The book showed one house in each state, designed by a prominent local architect. Oregon's solar example was designed by Pietro Belluschi, and it featured almost as much north-facing glass as south-facing.

Passive solar brought a welcome emphasis on better insulation, as well as a heightened requirement for thermally massive interior surfaces. In the dominant wood economy of the Pacific Northwest, plentiful thermal mass was a newcomer. Could thermal mass play a role in cooling as well as in providing solar heating during winters? Curious about developing a thorough understanding of passive cooling, I spent one sabbatical year (1981–82) examining the subject.

Climate data from Mexico indicated that the city of Colima in the small homonymous state had an average daily range of temperature and relative humidity during December and January that matched Eugene's in July and August. The focus of the investigation started by examining if people in Colima were using passive cooling techniques to cope with hot weather. Most people had blocks of ice delivered daily, for their iceboxes (refrigerators). Even when Eugene's hottest weather matched Colima's coolest, and while I walked the streets in shorts and sandals seeking shade, Colima's folks walked in the sun wearing light jackets. Cooling was not their problem in that season. It was an early and valuable lesson in the fallacy of an "international thermal comfort zone."

The explorations within the Spanish colonial architecture of Colima Centro, however, made evident the use of courtyards everywhere. Instead of a myriad of shading devices, most buildings had most of their windows open to a courtyard, and the surrounding arcades provided the shading. Upon entering these courtyards, two factors seemed particularly present: depth and vegetation (Fig. 8.2). After taking measurements for air temperature and global temperature, it became clear that thermal mass had a key role in the creation of such environments.

In these hot-day and cool-night months, the average daily range of temperature was about 30 F°.[3] In all these Spanish colonial masonry buildings, the thermal mass of the courtyard's floor and walls kept the "coolth" of the early morning into the hot early afternoon.[4] It also delayed the heat of the afternoon to the cooler evening, where such warmth was better received. The massive arcades had another characteristic: by day, there was always at least one arcade in the shade, and at least one in the sun. There was always a degree of choice.

Summer nighttime exposure of thermal mass for cooling is central to Hay's Skytherm system. This principle guided my colleague G.Z. "Charlie" Brown and me to design a small restaurant in Cottage Grove, Oregon that incorporated thermal mass in its concrete floor slab, and numerous 30-gallon barrels of water.[5] A culvert below the floor delivered nighttime cool air in summer, drawn up and out by wind-turbine ventilators. A large south-facing clerestory delivered winter sun to a shelf of water barrels, while lower south windows admitted sun to the eating area. A grape arbor protected these lower windows from summer sun, and sheltered additional tables *a la trattoria*.

In 1987, we designed an office building for an electric utility near Eugene, using forced nighttime ventilation in summer through hollow-core slabs of the floor and roof (Fig. 8.2).[6] Again, shading was performed by deciduous vines on south-facing trellises. Extensive interior surfaces of split-face striated concrete block provided exposed thermal mass for both summer night cooling and winter day solar heating.

Water

Courtyards continued to be the focus of my research in 1994, this time in Andalusia. An array of remote sensors helped to document courtyards' performance, and my partner Leonard Siqueiro helped with physical measurements. Córdoba is an obvious choice as a research base. It has an annual patio contest in May, *Concurso de Patios*, and publishes a map for tourists listing the address as well as showing the location of every contestant. Therefore, throughout the year, these patio owners can expect to occasionally find a visitor at their door.

Figure 8.2 Above: Courtyard heights vary from shallow to deep, Columns 1–3. Courtyard vegetation ranges from barren to full-grown trees, Rows A to D; Below: The Emerald People's Utility District office building near Eugene, Oregon. Deciduous vines shade the south façade. Winter sun finds ample interior thermal mass to store its warmth. That ample interior thermal mass also stores the coolth supplied by summer night ventilation.

Source: Diagram and photograph by author.

Córdoba's patios are both older and generally deeper vertically than Colima's. Many of them feature *toldos*, fabric covers that can be drawn closed for daytime shade, then drawn back for nighttime exposure to breeze and the sky. The vegetation is more profuse, with multiple pots hanging high on walls, and fruit trees and vines are abundant.

Trees, vines and *toldos* can provide courtyard shade, but the *toldo* seems to have a distinctly particular advantage: exposure. If the courtyard is to achieve cooling during the lower night temperatures, it needs direct exposure to the cool night sky. The courtyard floor radiates to the sky, and stays cool until the sun finds it the next day. The deeper the courtyard, the less sun reaches the floor. However, the *toldos* shade so thoroughly that courtyards are relatively dark by day. It is not a coincidence that in the hot summers of Andalusia, darkness is associated with coolth. This is very common in many cities with similar weather conditions in Spain – also in Argentina and other parts of Latin America.

And yet, despite the predominance of darkness, multiple hanging pots inhabit the courtyard with plants that seek the light and sun even on the hottest days. Watering these numerous pots is often done with a can attached to a long pole. After dipping the can into a bucket, pond or fountain, it is raised and then poured into each pot. Obviously, a great deal of water is spilled in this process. Both the walls and the courtyard floor get wet, and evaporative cooling results. The symbiotic nature between heat, darkness and water creates an ideal environment for both humans and vegetation. The typical Andalusian courtyard is *toldo*-shaded and cooled by evaporation by day, and further cooled by radiation by night. The courtyard and its surrounding building are passively tempered by the actions of its users.[7]

If compared with Hay's Skytherm system, the courtyard is that moist space between the panels and the mass, now magnificently expanded and inhabited. The Skytherm system asks its inhabitants to adjust the insulated panels, opening and closing them as the weather suggests. This is "thermal sailing," asking the passive building's occupants to be active to maintain comfort. Courtyard inhabitants have long understood this well.

Energy activism

My first years of teaching were also the peak years of resistance to the war in Vietnam. Activism was the *status-quo* in student life. The environmental movement flourished, and the impacts of energy generation became widely evident. Wasteful energy practices began to be scrutinized, and in 1970 Eugene delayed the construction of a nuclear power plant by public vote. With the campaign against the N-plant based on a questionable need for so much power, and the even more questionable destination of the resulting nuclear waste, Oregon spoke up. In the spring of 1970, the local election was accompanied by the first Earth Day and environmental control systems (ECS) concerns in the wider community enlivened the lecture hall.

The Eugene Water and Electric Board (EWEB) was shocked and angered by the defeat of their nuclear power plant, and it soon became obvious that someone pro-conservation should be elected for the board. I took on that challenge, and in 1972, while George McGovern was losing badly to Richard Nixon, I was elected to a four-year term. Electricity and water, more ECS, and a steep learning curve about supply and demand accompanied this new unpaid second job.

The Middle-East Oil Embargo hit just a few months after the election, and my message of conservation attracted attention. Governor Tom McCall appointed me to a newly formed Energy Conservation Advisory Committee. Resenting the fame that came with the position, business-oriented colleagues outvoted me 4–1 throughout my term. Halfway through this ordeal, the at-large seat on EWEB was up for election. The challenger was an environmental activist friend, Marian Frank; the incumbent, a building contractor, Calvin Schmidt. After a recount of some 28,000 votes, Frank lost by two votes. More than 40 years later, it remains the closest election in Eugene's history. EWEB soon abandoned plans for any large-scale energy generation, nuclear or not. Energy conservation rather than generation became the goal.[8]

In the late 1990s, two hot energy topics in Oregon were energy deregulation, severing the ties between energy generation and distribution, and public purpose funds, assessed on utility bills, to promote energy conservation and develop renewable electricity sources. Oregon Republicans supported deregulation, which was seen as a way to reduce energy costs through free market competition, while the Democrats supported public purpose funds. Neither party liked the other's favorite. With Democrats in control of the Governor's office and Senate, and Republicans running the House, neither of these ideas could pass without compromise.

Oregonians thus received both deregulation and public purpose funds in a 1999 restructuring bill. The Energy Trust of Oregon (ETO) was established to collect and administer funds for both energy efficiency and renewable electricity. Answerable to the Oregon Public Utility Commission, the ETO board was appointed in 2001. Thanks to my EWEB activism and years of teaching about efficiency and solar energy, I was appointed to the ETO board at the outset. Within a year we had hired a staff and commenced business.

ETO's funds came initially from a surcharge on the electric bills of the two major investor-owned electric utilities, PacificCorp and Portland General Electric. These two serve approximately two-thirds of Oregon's population. The 1999 restructuring legislation specified that 2.46 percent of their total billings go to ETO. Initially this amounted to some $45 million annually. Of that amount, 77 percent was spent on energy efficiency projects and the remaining 23 percent went toward generation of electricity from renewable sources. ETO was given 10 years of life, and we set ambitious goals: by 2012, achieve energy efficiency equivalent to 300 megawatts, and help Oregon to install 450 MW of renewable energy sources.

Impressed by our electricity savings, in 2003 Oregon's largest natural gas utility, Northwest Natural, asked the public utilities commission to decouple their rates from profits, while giving ETO 1.5 percent of their residential and commercial billings for energy efficiency investments. This ringing endorsement of our work, barely a year into our programs, enabled us to be fuel-neutral in our efficiency programs.

Dealing with both energy efficiency and renewable energy generation results in a fiscal split personality. For energy efficiency, we are limited to "cost-effective" investments, which means the cost of the technology has to be less than the marginal cost for the utility to provide another kilowatt hour of electricity (or therm of natural gas) to meet the demand on the utility system at a specific time. For renewable energy investments, we are limited to "above-market" costs. On one hand, we tell people interested in energy efficiency, "Your technology doesn't qualify unless it costs less than this"; on the other, we tell people interested in renewable energy, "We can't help you unless it costs more than this."

To my lasting chagrin as an architect and passive solar enthusiast, direct use of solar energy for anything other than making electricity is lumped under energy efficiency, limited to that "cost-effective" maximum. Daylighting, water heating, passive solar heating and passive cooling are considered efficiency rather than energy production. Thus, the ETO can give a residence or a business more per kilowatt-hour for a PV system than for the more efficient solar water heating system.

With an energetic, talented staff and consistent levels of funding, we soon established energy savings that surpassed the past efforts of the utilities, with their ambivalent attitude about conservation: "Fewer kilowatt-hours sold meant lower profits," they had said. Our renewable energy investments took somewhat longer to have an effect. Most of the initial money went to utility-scale wind farms east of the Columbia Gorge.

After the 2006 elections, Democrats controlled both houses of the Oregon legislature. The legislature enacted a Renewable Portfolio Standard (RPS), extended ETO's life to 2025 and mandated additional funds for energy efficiency. The RPS required utilities to fund large wind farms without ETO help, and ETO renewable funds, undiminished, are now capped at 20 MW per installation. We have invested in small wind, timber mill biomass, wastewater biomass, food waste biogas, dairy biogas, geothermal and small hydropower for irrigation districts. We have funded more than 100 MW of photovoltaic installations. For perspective, since the solar program began in 2003, Energy Trust has supported 300 times as many grid-tied solar electric systems as were installed in Oregon's entire prior history.

The ETO Board now has 13 members, nearly equal in gender and evenly spread geographically, ranging in age from early 30s to late 70s. Today, Oregon is moving steadily toward a sustainable energy economy, thanks to greatly increased efficiency and renewable energy production.

Notes

1 John S. Reynolds, Milt Larson and M. Steven Baker, "The Atypical Mathew Solar House at Coos Bay, Oregon," *Solar Energy* 19, no. 3 (1977): 219–232.
2 Edward Mazria, *The Passive Solar Energy Book* (Emmaus, PA: Rodale Press, 1979).
3 F° indicates temperature range, while °F indicates a single temperature reading.
4 Coolth is a term commonly used in passive energy design to define the absence of heat; the cooling equivalent of warmth.
5 John S. Reynolds and G.Z. Brown, "Commercial Building, Cottage Grove, Oregon." In *Encyclopedia of Architecture: Design, Engineering & Construction* 4, eds. Joseph A. Wilkes and Robert T. Packard (New York: Wiley, 1989), 475–476.
6 Robert Ashley and John S. Reynolds, "Overall and Zonal Energy End Use in an Energy Conscious Office Building," *Solar Energy Journal* 52, no. 1 (January 1994): 75–83.
7 John S. Reynolds, *Courtyards: Aesthetic, Social, and Thermal Delight* (New York: John Wiley & Sons, 2002).
8 John S. Reynolds, "Something of a Gadfly," *Journal of Architectural Education* 30, no. 3 (February 1977): 58–61.

9 Passive cooling systems in times of climate change

Pablo La Roche

It is clear that carbon emissions from buildings must be reduced to limit our anthropogenic effects on the environment. However, changing comfort aspirations and economic development have dramatically increased the number of mechanically cooled buildings in both residential and commercial buildings in developed and less developed countries.[1] Rapid population growth and urbanization in less developed countries have also been accompanied by the expansion of highly vulnerable urban communities living in informal settlements, many of which are on land exposed to extreme weather.[2] During extreme heat events, which are becoming more common in a warming climate,[3] inadequate building design and expensive energy make air conditioning prohibitive for low-income families. Furthermore, climate change is projected to increase energy demand for cooling in the residential and commercial sectors,[4] with negative health implications and increases in mortality and morbidity, especially for the elderly.[5]

A large body of research on sustainable architecture is directed to improving established technologies, such as HVAC systems, while making buildings tighter and better insulated.[6] However, there are other options. In his paper "Solarchitecture," Harold Hay advocated for the planning and construction of natural air-conditioned houses and proposed the integration of interdisciplinary fields involving natural radiation forces, building design, materials of construction, and human comfort.[7] Hay argued that solarchitecture could bring solar energy into residential use quicker and more economically than methods which have ignored this integration. As he used to say, it is not about getting more energy but about how to store it and keep it in place.[8] Passive architecture can harness this energy through smart building design, and passive cooling systems can transfer this heat from a building to various natural heat sinks, using heat flow paths that do not exist in conventional buildings. For example, a mechanically cooled building in a hot and dry climate is insulated to reduce heat gain from the hot summer day so that the air conditioner can operate more efficiently. However, with night ventilation, the building opens at night to cool its thermal mass and closes during the day, staying cooler for a longer period of time. A typical roof in a hot climate will also be insulated to reduce heat gains from the exterior, but this will not actually cool the building. In an operable roof pond, such as the Skytherm system developed by Hay, the roof is not insulated and the interior heat is transferred to water bags in the roof, which are then cooled by radiation to the night sky, reducing indoor air temperature. During the daytime, the roof pond is shaded to reduce solar gains while it absorbs energy from the building, keeping it cooler for a longer period. A roof pond system such as this one is not insulated and blocks or promotes energy flows as needed to maintain low indoor temperatures. In all cases, by including some thermal capacity and operability to control heat flows, the building's capacity to work with climate is augmented.

Because of how they collect, store, and distribute energy, passive cooling systems provide thermal comfort using a fraction of the energy used by conventional mechanical systems, achieving thermal comfort with lower capital and operating costs. Through their simple design, they can also be built at lower costs, using local labor and resources, as well as generating income that stays in the community, contributing to economic and social sustainability. They also provide opportunities for the occupant to establish closer connections with natural cycles and rhythms. Passive cooling systems benefit both the occupant and the planet.

Generally, all buildings are heated by solar radiation during the day and cooled during the night by convection and radiant loss to the sky. In warm climates, the average indoor temperature is usually higher than the outdoor average because heat gains are usually higher than losses. A passive cooling system can reduce indoor temperature by transferring heat from a building to various natural heat sinks.[9] Passive cooling systems are typically classified according to the heat sinks that they use to store energy: ambient air (sensible or latent), the upper atmosphere, water, and undersurface soil.[10] The applicability of a given cooling system is affected by multiple climate variables and not all systems can be used in all environments. This chapter will discuss the main features of several passive cooling systems developed by the author at the University of California Los Angeles and at Cal Poly Pomona University, both in California, USA. These systems are organized in three groups: cooling with air, cooling with water, and cooling with the sky. The research and development of these systems is a form of activism that defies conventional envelope construction in the search for new paradigms for cooling. The implementation of these systems in conventional practice should be promoted, with a positive effect on people, prosperity, and the planet.

Cooling with air

The atmosphere provides a powerful medium for heat transfer, primarily through convection. Cooling by ventilation to the atmosphere is probably the simplest way to remove heat from buildings, as comfort or night ventilation. Comfort ventilation provides direct well-being by air movement through the body, evaporating sweat and cooling the skin. Night ventilation cools the thermal mass of the building with outside air. During the daytime, the cooled mass acts as a heat sink, reducing the rate of indoor temperature rise. For night ventilation to be effective the building must have sufficient thermal mass, outside cool air must be brought inside at specific times, and night temperatures have to be low enough to cool the mass.

A microcomputer-controlled thermostat was developed at UCLA and evaluated at the Department of Architecture's Energy Lab.[11] This intelligent control system measured both indoor and outdoor temperature and used decision-based algorithms to operate a fan and maximize indoor thermal comfort using outdoor air. The controller turned the fan on and off as necessary to cool down the building's interior mass so that it could "coast" comfortably through the next day, reducing the need for air conditioning.

The test cells with the smart ventilation system always performed better than the test cells with a fixed infiltration rate. A higher air change rate increased the amount of cool air entering the space, lowering the temperature of the mass and also lowering the maximum temperature the next day. A lower value of comfort low reduced the indoor maximum temperature of the next day. Comfort low should be set at the minimum temperature tolerated by the occupants; in this case 18.3 °C (65 °F) was used. Tests confirmed that building design considerations affect system performance: shade, more mass, and higher volumes of controlled ventilation outperformed unshaded windows, less mass, and fixed ventilation rates. Various control strategies comparing these conditions were tested in the summers of 2000 and 2001. The control strategy that achieved the most hours in comfort and the lowest maximum temperatures is expressed in controller rule (1) below:

$$\text{If } t_o < t_i \text{ and } t_i > \text{Cf\_low and } t_i < \text{Cf\_high } \textit{then} \text{ fan ON else fan OFF} \quad (1)$$

Where:

To = temperature outside
Ti = temperature inside
Cf low = comfort low, lower limit of the comfort zone
Cf high = comfort high, upper limit of the comfort zone

Since this smart controller is temperature based and not time controlled, it can adjust the ventilation rate whenever exterior temperatures can provide cooling, during the day or night. Implementation of this simple rule based system would provide energy savings for buildings in different climates.

Further research expanded the implementation of night ventilation to combine it with green roofs. Results of research over several years at the Lyle Center for Regenerative Studies in Cal Poly Pomona, also with test cells, different types of plants, windows, and shading systems, consistently indicated that during the summer, a night-vented uninsulated green roof performed better than an insulated green roof and better than an insulated white roof, also night ventilated. The uninsulated green roof combined with night ventilation cools in two ways: (1) the green canopy layer reduces the effect of solar gains by reducing the sol–air temperature, and (2) the soil or growth medium acts as a heat sink when it is thermally coupled to the interior. Plants with a higher Leaf Area Index (LAI) and soil with higher density worked best.

Another study further developed the cooling potential of green roofs through the development of a variable-insulation green roof.[12] This also had 10 cm of insulation, but instead of being part of the green roof assembly, it rested on the ceiling between the air space and the roof construction. There were two openings in this ceiling, one of them with a small fan which could be turned on or off with the controller using rule (1). Typically, during cool summer nights, the fan is turned on, so that air circulates from the exterior into the interior and then to the plenum, cooling the thermal mass of the green roof from below. As the day gets warmer, the exterior fan is turned off while the plenum fan continues to circulate the air between the plenum and the space, transferring the heat from the space to the green roof substrate, which acts as a heat sink, keeping the space cooler for a longer period. During winter days when it is warmer inside than outside, the plenum fan is turned off, so that the air acts as an additional insulation layer. Thus, the plenum fan couples and decouples the green roof with the space below as required.

To test the system, four cells were monitored between 2011 and 2012. The first cell was a control, with a white-painted and code-compliant insulated roof. The other three cells had different types of green roofs: a non-insulated green roof laid above a metal plate, a green roof with 10 cm of insulation underneath, and the variable-insulation roof. In all series the variable-insulation green roof performed best, with values similar to the uninsulated green roof (Fig. 9.1).[13]

Uninsulated and variable insulation green roofs can be used when night temperatures are below 25 °C (77 °F) and daytime temperatures are below 40 °C (104 °F) with a daytime swing of at least 15 °C (27 °F). Figure 9.1 shows when variable-insulation green roofs can be used, following the thermal mass and night ventilation zone in Givoni and Milne's chart. Caution must be taken with uninsulated green roofs because the losses or gains during excessively warm or cold periods can exceed the savings provided. This research demonstrates that it is possible to use green roofs in a more powerful and effective way by combining natural ventilation with the thermal mass of a green roof as a heat sink.

Cooling with water

Even though their heat sink ultimately is the air, indirect and direct evaporative cooling systems are included in a separate section from the air because water is an important cooling and transport component of the system.

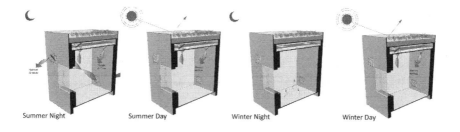

| Summer Night | Summer Day | Winter Night | Winter Day |

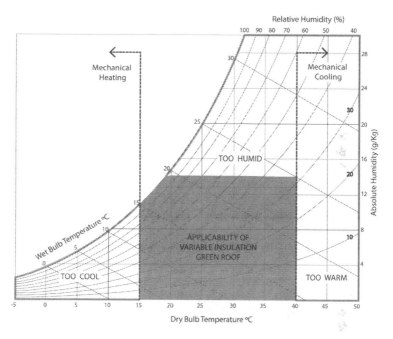

Figure 9.1 Above: Summer and winter cooling strategies in the variable-insulation green roof; Below: Climatic applicability of variable-insulation green roofs for cooling.

Source: Drawings by author.

Evaporative cooling is the process by which the sensible heat in an air stream is exchanged for the latent heat of water droplets or wetted surfaces. The sensible temperature of the air is reduced with an increase in humidity. This process is adiabatic, because overall, no energy is gained or lost in the air. Furthermore, the amount of heat absorbed by the evaporation of water – its latent heat – is very high compared to other modes of heat transfer, with the potential to significantly cool the air.

In hot and dry climates, evaporative cooling increases thermal comfort because it lowers the dry-bulb temperature closer to the comfort zone.

Evaporative cooling can be direct or indirect and is typically implemented through towers or ponds. In a direct evaporative cooling system, the air is cooled by evaporation of water and this humidified and cooled air is introduced into the building. In an indirect evaporative cooling system, a building component such as the ceiling absorbs heat inside the building. This heat is then transferred to the water (e.g., through embedded pipes), then pumped to a pond or tower where the water is cooled by evaporation, ultimately transferring the heat from the building to the air. According to Baruch Givoni, direct evaporative cooling can be implemented when wet bulb temperatures are below 22 °C (71.6 °F) and indirect evaporative cooling when wet bulb temperatures are below 24 °C (75.2 °F) with a maximum dry bulb temperature of 42 °C (107.6 °F).[14]

The author built and tested several indirect evaporative cooling systems using towers and roof ponds. With Givoni at UCLA, the author tested a roof pond with floating insulation cooled at night by sprays of water, based on Givoni's previous experiments.[15] Results demonstrated a direct relationship between the wet bulb temperature and the performance of the system; lower wet bulb temperatures were linked to lower indoor temperatures. At Cal Poly Pomona University, the author developed and tested another version of this roof pond in which the water spray was operated by a smart controller. Several rules were tested; the simplest one compared the temperature of a metal painted black surface facing the sky with the outside air temperature. If the temperature of the surface was lower than air temperature then the surface was radiating to the night sky and the pump was turned on. A more complex rule included the indoor temperature of the test cell and the water temperature; see controller rule (2) below.

If Tsurf(A) < Outdoortemp(A) + 2 & Roof pond(A) > Comfortlow & Twater(A) > lowatertemp then PUMP ON   (2)

where:

Tsurf(A) = temperature of the external metal plate
Outdoortemp(A) = outdoor dry bulb temperature
Roof pond(A) = temperature in the test cell with the roof pond
Comfortlow = lower limit of the comfort zone
Twater(A) = temperature of the water
lowatertemp = lowest minimum temperature of the water

Another roof pond developed by the author with Cal Poly Pomona students had fins that closed during the summer day and opened during the night. Still other configurations had fixed fins angled so that they blocked direct solar radiation during the daytime but permitted sky exposure during the night for radiant cooling.[16] These bodies of water can be located in exterior spaces such as gardens or courtyards and cool the building with a water-to-air heat exchanger (WAHE) or they can be located above the building, directly cooling the spaces below.

Students from the author's Cal Poly Pomona design studio, and with feedback from Corazon, a southern California NGO, and local residents, designed a community center for Tecate, Mexico, ten miles south of the border with the USA, in a high desert area with very hot and dry summers and cool winters.[17] The center has been built with volunteers from Corazon and the community, and includes low-cost passive systems, such as a solar attic and a direct evaporative cooling tower. It began operating in early 2017 and is providing skills training workshops for adults, daycare facilities, meeting spaces for the community, and volunteer housing (Fig. 9.2). Measurements in the downdraft evaporative cool tower demonstrated that it was able to cool the air from an outdoor temperature of 36.7 °C (98 °F)

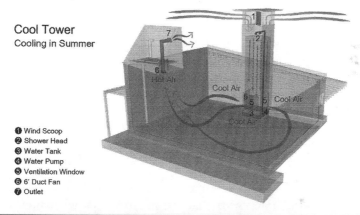

Figure 9.2 Downdraft evaporative cool tower with passive cooling strategies.
Source: Drawing and photograph by author.

and a RH 24 percent entering the tower to 20.8 °C (69.5 °F) and 100 percent RH exiting at the bottom of the tower inside the space. A 16 °C (28.5 °F) reduction of the outlet temperature of the air with no compressor cooling!

The goal is to continue developing these passive cooling systems so they can be fabricated at the community center and sold inexpensively for installation in new and existing buildings (currently none have heating or cooling). This will provide a source of income to the community while improving living conditions: true social, economic, and environmental sustainability. In these communities improving cooling performance is not a matter of saving energy; it is a matter of health. At the same time, projects such as this provide students with the opportunity to do good, while learning from practice.

Another study by the author and a postdoctoral student, Dongwoo Yeom, investigated the cooling potential of a green roof paired with a radiant cooling system in a hot and dry environment in southern California.[18] The green roof had pipes embedded in it, connected to a radiator inside the test cell. The radiator absorbed heat from the interior of the cell, which is dissipated through the green roof and the evaporative cooling during the irrigation. Unabsorbed excess water is recollected and reused. This configuration was monitored and compared with other cells in over forty series of tests over the summers of 2015 and 2016. The results demonstrated that this configuration maintained lower indoor temperatures than the other cells, including some with different types of green roofs. The best performance occurred when the radiant system pump operated continuously and the irrigation sprinkler operated twenty minutes per hour between 11:30 a.m. and 4:30 p.m. This demonstrates the potential for irrigation implementation in non-traditional ways that can improve thermal comfort and reduce energy consumption in buildings, while reducing the urban heat island effect.

Another series of experiments tested WAHEs combined with green roofs.[19] In this case the heat sink was a pond with a floating insulating panel and nighttime water spray. The heat from the interior that could not be absorbed by the green roof was transferred to the pond – the heat sink, and then dissipated into the atmosphere using the nighttime water spray. The results of the WAHE were promising. As expected, the amount of heat exchanged between the water and the air in the underwater pipe increases with the length of the pipe. The best performing length was the longest (11.4 feet), keeping the indoor temperature of the experimental cell below 27 °C (80.6 °F) during the daytime, while the ambient temperature was above 36 °C (96.8 °F). Higher air velocities in the pipe provided more cool air into the test cell and increased the overall system efficiency. However, an air speed beyond a certain value can also lead to a reduction in cooling. Larger pipe diameters increased the amount of cool air entering the cell and the system performance. Best results were obtained with a four-inch-diameter aluminum pipe. In addition, the higher the underwater pipe's thermal conductivity value, the greater the potential for cooling. This system provides opportunities to cool buildings or spaces with bodies of water.[20]

As part of his Master's thesis, Brandon Gullotti, a graduate student at the Lyle Center for Regenerative Studies, tested a system that used a strategy similar to the Trombe wall, but substituted the opaque thermal mass wall with a transparent water-wall.[21] The thickness of the water-wall was designed for optimal visual clarity to the outdoors and maximum volumetric heat capacity, and used hydronic heat exchange to move water on demand to an isolated storage tank. A flat-plate collector acted as a secondary, isolated gain system for heating and cooling, storing heat during the day and releasing it at night. The system was tested at the Lyle Center for Regenerative studies and demonstrated significant cooling potential.

As part of his PhD dissertation in 2017, Eric Carbonnier conducted research on fluid-based windows, introducing a highly conductive gap medium inside windows using 10-mm Ø Al2O3 nanoparticles dispersed in deionized water to enhance thermal conductivity. The solution harnessed the photothermal properties of Al2O3 nanofluids to trap, store, and transport thermally charged fluids to heat exchangers to preheat air, water, and generate electricity forming the Nanowindow. Carbonnier tested seven Nanowindow prototypes with varying air and fluid columns coupled with three different heat exchangers and a thermoelectric generator. His research confirmed that the optimal order of air and nanofluid (Al2O3) column favored the nanofluid close to the outdoor environment, exhibiting U-Factor's ranging from 0.39–0.49, and a Solar Heat Gain Coefficient (SHGC) of 0.43–0.670, which are comparable to double-pane window systems and meet energy code requirements. In heat exchange experiments, Nanowindow's convective and radiative heat coefficient outperformed baseline water filled windows by 8 percent and 22 percent. Thermoelectric generators converted the $0.093m^2$ of Nanowindow to produce a rated voltage of 0.31VDC/0.075ADC at standard test condition (STC). The potential for window gap technology to shift from resisting energy to harnessing solar energy presents a unique opportunity to turn windows into transparent generators. This type of research opens new possibilities, in which windows change from conductive, transparent, and leaky building elements to transparent generators of energy that would also store and transfer energy as required.

Cooling with the sky

The sky provides the ultimate continuous heat sink to maintain the Earth's thermal equilibrium. All bodies radiate and absorb energy to the sky at the same time, usually at different rates and wavelengths. Any ordinary surface that "sees" the sky loses heat by emitting longwave radiation. These radiant heat losses take place during the day and night, but only at night, when there are no solar gains, are the heat losses to the sky higher than the heat gains and the building can actually be cooled. A rule of thumb for a location with clear days and nights is that radiative cooling has a potential rate of about 10 percent of the summer radiative heating rate.[22] One of the first contemporary radiant cooling systems, Skytherm, was developed by Hay in 1978.[23]

Radiant systems could be implemented in developing countries, in which a large portion of the population lives in informal settlements with minimum access to basic living conditions. In these, a common initial stage of the homes starts with metal sheets in walls and roofs, replaced by brick and concrete when the family has sufficient financial resources.[24] These metal roofs are very hot during the daytime but cool down quickly in the evening as they radiate energy to the night sky. In 1996, Baruch Givoni, Carlos Gomez, and Anthony Gulish, at UCLA, developed a radiant cooling system for use in these buildings.[25]

The author conducted additional tests with variations of this system.[26] During the daytime the panels were closed to form a continuous radiant barrier and reduce the heat flow into the interior. During the night, the panels were opened into a vertical position, enabling radiant and convective heat flow from the interior space to the metal ceiling, which is then cooled by longwave radiation to the sky. The rotation of the insulating ceiling panels between the closed and vertical positions was achieved by an electromechanical system designed and built by Antulio Gomez at UCLA. In a real home the panels could easily be controlled manually from the interior (e.g., by a rope). Interior operable insulation panels are not exposed to the wind and the rain, and thus can be simpler in construction, lighter, and much less expensive than external operable panels.

These experiments and research evaluate the performance of the systems, but the actual architectural development and expression can be very different as long as the heat flow paths are understood and considered appropriately. An example is the Xylem, developed at CallisonRTKL that provides additional outdoor thermal comfort while mitigating the heat island effect[27] (Fig. 9.3). The Xylem proposes to improve outdoor thermal comfort by implementing a vegetated roof and water circulation for radiant cooling in addition to shading and natural ventilation. This concept is based on the author's research in passive cooling but takes a form that is appropriate to the architectural concept being developed.

It is important to continue developing and improving the performance of passive cooling systems with new technologies and materials now available, always using alternate paths to harness energy flows and creating buildings that are simpler to operate and more resilient. Hay was a believer in science and basic principles. This chapter has outlined some alternative paths investigated by the author to develop passive cooling technologies that use simple systems to provide low-energy cooling. However, there is much more to be done and there is little time.

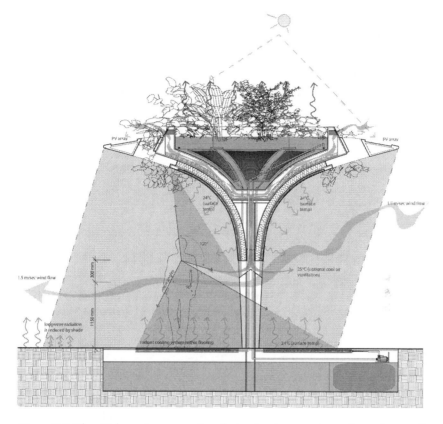

Figure 9.3 The Xylem. An example of the implementation of passive cooling
 concepts.

Source: Image courtesy of CallisonRTKL.

Notes

1 Harold Wilhite, "The conditioning of comfort," *Building Research and Information*
   37, no. 1 (2009): 84–88.
2 Field, C.B., V.R. Barros, D.J. Dokken, K.J. Mach, M.D. Mastrandrea, T.E. Bilir,
   M. Chatterjee, K.L. Ebi, Y.O. Estrada, R.C. Genova, B. Girma, E.S. Kissel, A.N.
   Levy, S. MacCracken, P.R. Mastrandrea, and L.L. White (eds.), *Contribution of
   Working Group II to the Fifth Assessment Report of the Intergovernmental Panel
   on Climate Change* (Geneva, Switzerland: World Meteorological Organization,
   2014), 47.
3 Ibid., 42.
4 Ibid., 19.
5 Ibid.
6 Energy codes typically propose more insulation and tighter envelopes to reduce
   energy consumption. Standards such as Passivhaus also require high levels of

insulation in walls and windows, with an airtight building envelope, and ventilation provided with a highly efficient heat or energy recovery system. While these strategies are effective, there are other options such as passive cooling, which are usually not considered sufficiently.

7 Harold R. Hay, "Energy, technology, and solarchitecture," *Mech. Eng.* 95, no. 11 (1973): 18–22.

8 Testimony from Margot McDonald and others who worked closely with Hay.

9 Baruch Givoni, *Passive Low Energy Cooling of Buildings* (New York: John Wiley & Sons, 1994), 3.

10 Ibid.

11 Pablo La Roche and Murray Milne, "Effects of window size and mass on thermal comfort using an intelligent ventilation controller," *Solar Energy* 77 (2004): 421–434.

12 Pablo La Roche, "Keeping comfortable with green roofs: experimental series in Southern California," presented at the CitiesAlive 11th Annual Green Roof and Wall Conference, San Francisco, USA (October 2013).

13 Pablo La Roche and Umberto Berardi, "Comfort and energy savings with active green roofs," *Energy and Buildings* 82 (2014): 492–504.

14 Baruch Givoni, *Climate Considerations in Building and Urban Design* (New York: John Wiley & Sons, 1998), 42–44.

15 Pablo La Roche and Baruch Givoni, "Indirect evaporative cooling with an outdoor pond," *Passive Low Energy Architecture Conference PLEA 2000, Architecture City and the Environment* (Cambridge, UK: Proceedings of the Solar Conference, no. 25, 2000), 603–608.

16 Rudy Marnich, Rob Yamnitz, and Pablo La Roche, "Shaded Modular Roof Pond for Passive Cooling in Hot–Dry Climates," *Building Enclosure Sustainability Symposium, BESS 2010 Conference* (2010).

17 Corazon is a non-profit organization based in southern California that has been working in Mexican border cities since 1978, building community by strengthening families, enabling service, promoting self-sufficiency, and inspiring mutually beneficial relationships across borders.

18 Dongwoo Yeom and Pablo La Roche, "Investigation on the cooling performance of a green roof with a radiant cooling system," *Energy and Buildings* 149 (2017): 26–37.

19 Umberto Berardi, Pablo La Roche, and Jose Manuel Almodovar, "Investigation on the cooling performance of a green roof with a radiant cooling system," *Energy and Buildings* 151 (2017): 406–417.

20 Pablo La Roche, Jose Manuel Almodovar, and Dongwoo Yeom, "Cooling with water and green roofs: passive systems to improve thermal comfort," *Façade Tectonics World Congress* (Los Angeles, CA: 2016): 269–276.

21 Brandon Gullotti and Pablo La Roche, "Novel Water-Wall Envelope Component for Passive and Active Cooling," *American Solar Energy Society Conference ASES Solar 2015* (July 28–30, 2015).

22 Jeffrey Cook, *Passive Cooling* (Cambridge, MA: The MIT Press, 1989), 606.

23 However, the investigations that led him to the full development of the system started in the 1940s with his prototypes on movable insulation in India.

24 This process is typical of housing in developing countries. Families in Brazil's favelas or Venezuela's barrios quickly build a basic shelter to take ownership of a piece of land, but they begin to modify and expand it immediately with new materials.

25 To test the system, they built a test cell in UCLA's Department of Architecture energy lab. Internal dimensions were 1.00 m × 1.00 m × 0.95 m, and walls and floor were super-insulated with polyurethane panels 80 mm (3.5 in.) thick. The projected area of the gabled-sloped metal roof was 1.16 m × 1.60 m. The roof was not insulated and was painted white, effectively converting it into a nocturnal radiator. Centrally hinged, lightweight, and operable reflecting panels below it regulated the heat gains and losses through the roof, opening or closing as required.

26 Pablo La Roche and Baruch Givoni, "The effect of heat gain on the performance of a radiant cooling system", *Passive Low Energy Architecture Conference PLEA in Toulouse, France* (2002).

27 Pablo La Roche, *Carbon Neutral Architectural Design* (Abingdon: CRC Press, 2017), 190.

10 Actively stretching passive

Adventures with night roof spray cooling

Richard (Dick) Bourne

This chapter describes an engineer/entrepreneur's intermittent efforts, beginning in 1979, to develop and market a highly cost-effective cooling system now called NightSky, that has significant future opportunities. It suggests that passive design inventions sometimes need to become hybrid using one or more active components to enhance performance and reduce maintenance requirements such that widespread marketing is possible. This approach seems particularly necessary to maximize the market potential for technologies that use the roof to create "natural" climate control in buildings.

In 1975, I was an Associate Professor of Construction Management at the University of Nebraska/Lincoln (UNL) and had been studying the solar energy work of others, including that of Harold Hay. His excellent contribution with John I. Yellott pioneered the development of solar roof ponds in the Southwest and was compelling for its focus on passive design.[1] But in Nebraska's more severe climate, I began to forge a different path focused on the needs of electric utilities toward managing the operating times of heating and cooling systems for buildings. In 1974, the Lincoln Electric System (LES) supported the design, construction, and monitoring of what became the UNL/LES Solar Home. This project was a solar hybrid, placing an air-source electric heat pump in an attic with south-facing (solar) glazing. Paired with a large below-floor insulated water tank, the heat pump could operate at its most favorable times: at night in the cooling season, with the attic fully vented, and during daytime in the heating season, with the attic vents closed during solar conditions. Tank water pre-conditioned by the heat pump was circulated through a fan coil to heat or cool the house. It was unique among the solar demonstrations of the time, and so I did not embellish the work of Hay until our family relocated to Davis, California in 1978.

The first California summer spurred intrigue with the possibilities for non-compressor cooling. The NightSky concept emerged as our flat-roofed house rekindled thoughts from Hay's Skytherm system.[2] After conceptual work I built a prototype of a night roof-spray ("NRS") cooling system with a 3" water layer over the garage.[3] The concept combined the power of evaporative and night radiant cooling instead of relying on radiant sky cooling alone, as Hay had demonstrated. The water layer was contained in a shallow membrane-lined "bathtub" created with perimeter framing on the un-insulated roof. Styrofoam 2'x4' panels floated on the water layer, glued down by water adhesion, eliminating worries of lift-off in high-wind conditions. A ¼"-thick cement topping prevented UV-damage to the foam. A small pump sprayed water (from below) over the panels at night to cool the water, which then flowed back through the panel joints and remained below the insulated panels in the daytime (Fig. 10.1).

Schematic Prototype

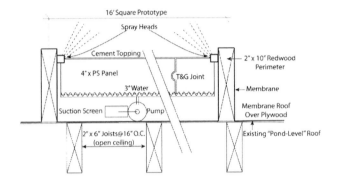

Demonstration Project

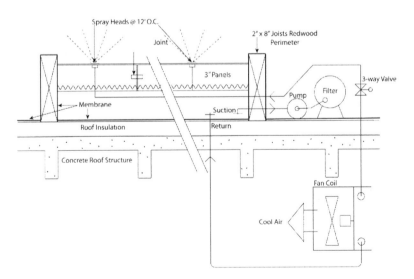

Figure 10.1 Above: Schematic prototype; Below: Schematic demonstration project. Source: Drawings by author.

Completed in 1982, the system worked effectively, keeping the garage below 80 °F on 100 °F afternoons. We tested performance one evening in July by capturing spray water at dusk on a large plastic sheet and quickly measuring the bulk water temperature. The water was 49 °F when the air temperature was 68 °F. This "cooler-than-wet bulb" result made clear the value of radiant cooling to the clear sky. We ran the prototype system manually on most summer nights, and after a few summers we were convinced that the system had potential and was worth a greater time investment.

Nurtured by California

In 1979, I had started the Solar Concept Development Company and by 1980 had met future partners: Marshall Hunt and Dave Springer. From the company, we formed the Davis Energy Group (DEG) in 1981 as a solar and energy efficiency consulting firm working in product development, HVAC design, and building energy analysis. A NRS improvement opportunity appeared in 1987 with the California Energy Commission's Energy Technologies Advancement Program grants, and DEG successfully petitioned for support to further develop the NRS system, relabeled as the Cool Storage Roofs (CSR) concept, a non-residential building cooling technology. The project ran from 1989 to 1992 and included design, development, performance simulation, a large demonstration, and data-based calibration.

In design and development phases, we determined that the commercially available cement-topped panels used in the prototype, available only in a 2'x4' size, were less cost-effective than 4'x8' by 3"-thick extruded Styrofoam panels. In addition, we found a white panel coating that promised to be durable and UV-resistant. We slotted all four panels' edges and inserted Styrofoam splines so that they would stay together and transfer support to adjacent panels under foot traffic and wind. A 6,300-square-foot demonstration was built on a warehouse at the California Office of State Printing near downtown Sacramento. It included a sand filter with an automatic backwash cycle to remove dirt and assure that spray heads would not clog. In addition, we designed an optimized spray system with piping in the water layer below the panels, and spray heads located on a 12' grid pattern in the panels. And lastly, we developed a computerized control system with an algorithm that based its nightly target water temperature and spray start time on the prior day's weather.[4]

The one-story warehouse was an ideal site for the demonstration project because it had been built with a "dead-level" roof, strong enough to become a future second floor. The building was occupied in part by drivers on fork-lift trucks, moving pallets of paper and printed goods, so the roll-up doors were frequently open. Despite the roof's 2" rigid insulation layer, its underside reached such high summer daytime temperatures that the space below was too warm for comfort. We installed a large custom fan coil in the most occupied area to deliver cooling from the CSR water.

After completion in August 1991, the system operated during a September that conveniently included 15 days with highs above 100 °F, with an average EER of 39; about four times the average efficiency of a conventional 1990s-era rooftop cooling unit. Data-based full-summer simulations highlighted the system's potential cost-effectiveness, with estimated paybacks of one to five years on a variety of commercial and institutional building types in California.

How and how well?

The NRS cooling mechanisms rely on spraying water across a relatively horizontal plane facing a clear night sky. Both radiative and evaporative cooling mechanisms come into play.[5] As the night proceeds, the ambient air becomes cooler. Sky-facing surfaces keep cooling radiatively as moisture condenses on them.[6] After condensation starts, radiation increases because there is even less moisture in the air. This is why the most efficient time to spray cool water on a roof is just before dawn – when the air is coolest and driest.

When water is sprayed uniformly at night above a horizontal surface facing the clear sky, the two cooling mechanisms work synergistically. The water is cooled evaporatively if it is warmer than the wet-bulb temperature of the surrounding air, and it is also cooled radiatively as the droplets send heat through the clear sky. Since the NRS goal is to collect the water cooled in this combined process, droplets should be large enough so they land for collection, instead of misting away to cool the great outdoors. Irrigation spray heads are ideal for this application. On a typical summer night, there is more evaporative cooling of the water at the start of the spray cycle, and more radiative cooling at the end.

As we tested, monitored, and then calibrated our model, we developed the following two rules-of-thumb for optimized NRS design:

1. spray rate of ~1 gallon/minute per 100 square feet of roof
2. water depth of ~3" (or two gallons per square foot of roof spray area) to store a full night's cooling capability with about 8 °F daily temperature range

During summer, with daily highs of 100 °F and lows in the mid-60s °F, the NRS system can store about 250 BTUs of cooling per square foot in a full night's operation – roughly twice what can be achieved with a radiation-only system. For a 2,000-square-foot one-story building, the 500,000 BTUs of cooling storage per night can typically provide full day comfort without a compressor. Compared to a closed water container, the "open" water configuration also simplifies design, since the liner can double as the water containment/roofing layer, and excess water in rainy season is easily drained away from the insulation-covered "bathtub."[7]

Add venture to passive

Serendipitously, a Davis-based business incubator called the Technology Development Center (TDC) was being formed in 1992, just as the CSR R&D project was wrapping up.[8] Charles Soderquist, an "angel investor" funding the TDC, was enthusiastic enough about the CSR technology to welcome it into the center and to invest in its start-up. With the product now named CoolRoof, Roof Science Corporation (RSC) was launched. RSC hired Thomas McKean, an enthusiastic young UC Davis MBA, to run the start-up company, and recruited a board team that included several experienced commercial construction industry business owners.[9]

Since low-rise commercial buildings typically have large flat roofs and large cooling loads, we decided to market first to the new commercial market segment. The most significant (and ultimately mistaken) board decision was to only offer a water-on-the-roof version. This original concept, the only one we had actually tested, is the most passive of the storage location options; a more active choice would cool water on the roof but store it down below.[10] Figure 10.2 diagrams the difference between water storage locations on-the-roof and off-the-roof.

From a technical standpoint, off-roof storage is better for commercial buildings, because it is more active, hence more controllable. The basic water-on-the-roof version passively delivers cooling continuously and

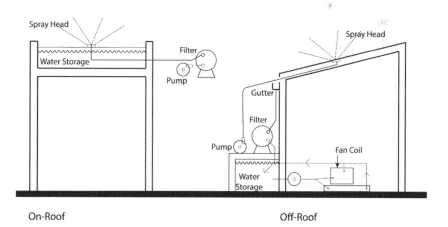

On-Roof   Off-Roof

Figure 10.2 Schematic comparison of on- and off-roof storage.
Source: Drawing by author.

uncontrollably downward through the ceiling, and naturally keeps the building cooler in the morning, with gradually rising water and indoor temperatures through the day. With cool water stored instead in an insulated tank, a room thermostat turns on a pump that circulates water to cool the space. To deliver cooling from the stored water, the active system uses additional pump energy compared to the water-on-the-roof alternative. But it is often more efficient overall because improved temperature control can reduce daily heat gains, which depend on the indoor/outdoor temperature difference. A passively cooled building gains more heat when it is cooler than needed in the morning and early afternoon, and this added cooling load can result in higher auxiliary cooling energy use.

In 1992 and 1993, RSC presented detailed design and performance studies to design teams for five major projects. Despite projected paybacks of less than three years, no team took a chance on the system. Soon the start-up funds were gone, Thomas McKean took another job, and RSC went idle. Over the years, only three more projects were completed with the passive system: a small test building at the University of Nebraska-Omaha,[11] and two two-story residential projects in Davis – one for the Bourne family, and the other a cooperative housing project.

We Bournes lived in the NRS-cooled home built on Isle Royale Lane, from spring 1994 through August 2012. The house was featured on the Peter Jennings show in 2001, in local newspapers, and in *Sunset Magazine* (September 2001). It is a rare Sacramento Valley house that has been comfortably cooled without a compressor.[12] On days when the outdoor temperature reached 105 °F, we seldom reached 80 °F indoors; in typical summer weather with highs in the upper 90s °F and lows in the lower 60s °F, the indoor high is typically 76 °F, with a morning low of 69 °F. The smart controller adjusts the length and start time of the NRS cycle to maintain ideal summer comfort without an indoor thermostat. Our neighbors were spending as much as $300 per month to stay at 80 °F through the summer, and we were paying less than $5/month for pump energy to maintain a daily average temperature of about 73 °F.

Unfortunately, as Hay also experienced, selling water-on-the-roof cooling is difficult. This mostly passive version requires more interaction between occupants and their home than many households are willing to devote. Cooling breezes arrived on most summer evenings, so we opened windows and our large vent port above the second floor, and then closed up in the morning. Most neighbors, meanwhile, were on autopilot, keeping windows closed and air-conditioners running.

New life with off-roof storage

The year 1993 brought the first off-roof storage project, when PG&E's ACT^2 program added a 7330-square-foot retrofit commercial building in Auburn,

CA and awarded project implementation to DEG. CoolRoof was selected as a cost-effective technology.[13] The retrofit system added a roof-spray mechanism, a 10,000-gallon buried fiberglass tank, revised roof drainage into the tank, a tank overflow drain, and cooling coils installed in the two existing rooftop cooling units. The project was monitored for two years and showed 55 percent cooling energy savings compared to the base case system.

After a two-year dry spell, 1996 breathed new life into what originated as CoolRoof. We had lost our product name to a California cool roofs' initiative for white-coated roofs, so beginning in 1994 we marketed as WhiteCap. The incentive came from two additional investors, and from prior contacts with energy-efficiency decision-makers in California's Department of General Services (DGS) and the United States Federal Energy Management Agency (US FEMA). The 1996 DGS project was a new Employment Development Department (EDD) building in South Central Los Angeles. Design documents were already complete, preventing full WhiteCap integration. We were able to add the most crucial components: roof spray system, buried storage tank, modified roof drains, radiant floor tubing, cooling coils, cooling delivery piping, filter, pumps, and microprocessor controls. The building is conditioned by rooftop heat pumps, to which we added cooling coils. After completion, operation, and monitoring, data-based projections showed 54 percent cooling energy savings.

The 1996 FEMA project was a retrofit on a U.S. Customs Station in Nogales, AZ. This project was the first to use an above-ground insulated storage tank. This wood-framed reservoir was built on an available exterior slab near the air-handler, to which we added a large pre-cooling coil. During two months of monitoring by the Pacific Northwest National Laboratory, the system achieved an average EER of 149.

The best yet

The year 1998 saw the completion of the All-Weather factory in Vacaville, CA. This new building included an attractive one-story "barrel-roof" office projecting from the 24' tall tilt-up concrete factory walls. The owner, Lance Porter, was intrigued by the WhiteCap concept and did not want rooftop units on the factory roof that would require long ductwork to serve the office. We offered and installed a full HVAC system with a buried 8,000-gallon tank in the front yard near the mechanical room, an air-cooled chiller serving as cooling backup, a pool heater as the heating source, combined radiant floor plus fan coil cooling and heating delivery, and smart controls. Instead of the 23 tons of rooftop units required to serve the 6,300-square-foot offices, we included a 10-ton auxiliary chiller programmed to operate at night for supplemental cooling of the tank when necessary. The cost savings from this reduction in cooling tonnage helped pay for WhiteCap components.

The All-Weather system continues to provide exemplary performance. It was monitored by PG&E for the 1998–99 summers, during which it demonstrated 73 percent cooling energy savings and 87 percent peak demand reduction compared to the base case rooftop units. The project won the ASHRAE Western Region design award in 1999.[14] Lance Porter joined the RSC Board of Directors and subsequently became a driving force in the company. The controls were developed and implemented by Paul Passantino of Performance Controls; he also joined the board, participating in the product and company name changes to NightSky and Integrated Comfort, Inc. (ICI). Passantino bought shares of departing investors in 2001 and became President and CEO.

Under Passantino's command another highly successful NightSky system was installed in 2002, on the Carnegie Institution's Global Ecology Center at Stanford University. The system was engineered by Rumsey Engineers, marking the first NRS system not designed by the author or the Davis Energy Group. This was also the first installation on a sloping-roof building, and the only one to date using a pre-assembled mechanical module that includes pumps, filter, heater, key plumbing and valves, and microprocessor controls. The module was pre-fabricated under Passantino's direction at the ICI shop. Like the All-Weather project, the Global Ecology Center delivers cooling both through radiant floors and fan coils, with the floors providing steady "baseload cooling" and the fan coils maintaining precise control in response to zone thermostats. Monitoring results showed 72 percent cooling energy savings for the project, which has been heralded as one of the highest-efficiency HVAC systems in any LEED-rated building.[15]

In 2003, limited ICI resources caused a halt to NightSky marketing efforts. Nonetheless, two more projects have been completed: the 2013 Parkview Place apartment building in Davis, and the 2015 UC Davis Solar Decathlon entry. ICI has stayed alive and prospered based not on NightSky but on a patented, retrofittable cooling product for commercial rooftop units, called DualCool.[16]

Parkview Place

In 2009, the Bournes, joined by three other senior couples, started the Parkview Place owner-occupied retirement project in Davis. Our goal, now accomplished, was to live in a downtown, all-electric "net-zero" apartment building. We were fortunate to acquire a corner lot a half-block from Central Park, with excellent sky access. We hired Mike Corbett, developer of the internationally acclaimed Village Homes solar neighborhood in Davis, as our designer/builder. Corbett's design sense and knowledge of city politics were instrumental in fulfilling our shared dream for the three-story building. Energy systems include ground-coupled heat pumps, radiant floor heating and cooling, and a photovoltaic array large enough to generate a 15 percent electricity surplus over our first three years of occupancy. The project also includes a synergistic NightSky configuration that combines rainwater collection and PV washing with cooling. While the original two NightSky patents had expired by 2016, US patent #9,257,938 B2 now covers this three-way combination. This concept has been used on both Parkview Place and the UC Davis 2015 Solar Decathlon house that took seventh place in the international competition.[17]

At Parkview Place, we built in an inexpensive underground 11,000-gallon membrane-lined rainwater collection tank that doubles as the NightSky cool storage reservoir. About 7" of annual rainfall is enough to fill the tank. At the 30-gallon/minute roof spray rate, all water drains through a filter into the tank. When the rainfall rate exceeds the filter's capacity, excess rainwater overflows into the geothermal boreholes, enhancing their performance. While the NightSky system loses some water to evaporation, the sky-radiative cooling does not result in water loss. A full season of NightSky cooling uses less than half of the rainwater storage, so no water needs to be purchased. The mineral-free rainwater minimizes system maintenance.

Bright future?

Prospects for future NightSky success are enhanced by the world's commitment to renewable energy sources, with photovoltaics (PV) clearly being one of the most compelling renewable options for buildings. PV synergy with NightSky cooling is significant since soiled PV arrays lose efficiency. Windblown dust lands on PV panels, and nightly condensation captures the dust, which cooks onto the panel surface, day after day, as the sun dries the dew. Fifteen percent PV performance reduction is common after as little as three weeks of exposure in these climates, where summer rainfall is rare. Various PV-washing technologies and services are now available, but none is as capable or cost-effective as the nightly washing offered by the NightSky system.

In addition to using PV washing to reduce the necessary size of the solar array, NightSky cost-effectiveness is enhanced by using:

1. the roof and roof drain systems as the crucial heat exchange surface, requiring just an inexpensive UV-resistant roof spray system to complete the cooling apparatus
2. low-cost underground or above-ground water storage in membrane-lined, site-built tanks that double as rainwater collection tanks
3. where auxiliary cooling is necessary, down-sized chillers that operate steadily and efficiently to further cool the storage water, reducing and consolidating tonnage, thus reducing first and maintenance costs compared to conventional rooftop cooling units
4. off-peak auxiliary operation to improve chiller efficiency and operate at times when summer electric rates are lowest.

The bottom line is that these synergies make NightSky extremely cost-effective for the future's net-zero buildings. There is a major opportunity for young and energetic leaders or organizations to finally carry this promising technology across the "Valley of Death" into the mainstream marketplace for low-rise buildings. However, entrepreneurs attempting this task face enduring hurdles, including convincing potential "early adopters" and regulators that NightSky systems:

1. have very favorable economics when fully integrated
2. facilitate net-zero buildings by reducing required PV area
3. fully or partially eliminate rooftop HVAC equipment, reducing roof maintenance issues and maximizing PV potential
4. deserve major payments from electric utilities for peak demand reduction
5. outlast, and have lower maintenance costs than, conventional HVAC systems.

Summary

This biographical narrative has presented the development of a concept that began in 1978, inspired by the work of Harold Hay. The concept has been modified and improved over the intervening years, evolving in the natural way in which it originally emerged from knowledge of Hay's Skytherm house. While Skytherm needed intelligent (and active) operation of a moving insulation cover over the contained water mass, NightSky uses a pump, also an active feature, instead of the moving covers; and NightSky doubles the cooling rate by facilitating evaporative cooling as well as radiant. In the end, it appears that an even more active NightSky version that stores water off the roof is the most commercially viable approach. Perhaps the most vital NightSky lessons are the same ones that emerged from the Skytherm House experience: those focusing on using passive, natural forces are the best starting point, but those changing energy-intensive conventional practices require active creativity and resilience, and a continual willingness to add intelligent active features to maximize market potential. This form of resiliency is too little discussed yet critically necessary for success. NightSky continues to be an active resilient system, yet clearly on the passive side of the cooling options continuum. NightSky remains full of potential for future entrepreneurs; after all, THE SKY IS THE LIMIT!

Notes

1 Harold R. Hay and John I. Yellott, "International aspects of air conditioning with movable insulation," *Solar Energy* 12, no. 4 (December 1969): 427–430, IN1, 431–438.

2 Hay's Skytherm House in Atascadero, CA used large sealed water bags on a membrane-lined, uninsulated steel ceiling deck, with movable insulation panels above. See Chapter 2 in this volume for full house details.

3 The garage became very warm in summer as it was the only un-insulated portion of our roof.

4 We had determined that the most efficient time to spray was just at dawn, when outdoor and clear sky temperatures are lowest. We programmed the spray cycle to extend further back in the night as cooling conditions became more extreme.

5 In dry climates, the clear night sky is the coldest location in the outdoor environment; the large daily temperature range is a result of an atmosphere containing little moisture. In daytime, incoming solar radiation faces less interference from moisture in the atmosphere, so the earth-surface environment warms rapidly. Conversely at night, outgoing radiation from sky-facing surfaces causes rapid cooling and much lower morning temperatures on the earth's surface. Radiation is a very powerful heat transfer mechanism, and in dry climates the night sky reaches sub-freezing temperatures as a radiative receiver.

6 The Psychrometric Chart (the HVAC engineer's reference of choice) clearly shows this principle; the cooling of air without moisture change shows up on the chart as leftward movement toward the saturation line; cooling beyond this point results in downward movement along the saturation line, to a lower moisture level; i.e. condensation on the nearest cool surface.

7 Designs with a closed water container on the roof/ceiling deck require a sealed membrane under the bag that protects the building from leakage and that drains rain water.

8 The TDC was started by Charles Soderquist (later a University of California Regent) and Mary Ferguson, who developed the concept while an MBA student at UC Davis.

9 The Board included: Mary Ferguson and Charles Soderquist of the TDC; John Beattie, president of Hester Roofing, a major commercial roofing contractor; Dan Ramos, Vice-President of a Sacramento commercial building developer; and the author.

10 Cooling thermal energy can most easily be stored below in a large water tank, but there are other possibilities including concrete slabs and phase-change materials.

11 In the late 1980s Dr. Bing Chen of the UNO Engineering Technology faculty spearheaded the design and construction of a test CSR on a small R&D building at the Allwine Prairie Reserve near Omaha.

12 Peter Whitely, "A laboratory for climate control," accessed January 1, 2018, www.questia.com/magazine/1G1-79828394/a-laboratory-for-climate-control.

13 Verifone project, accessed January 1, 2018, http://aceee.org/files/proceedings/1998/data/papers/0106.PDF.

14 The American Society of Heating, Refrigeration, and Air-Conditioning Engineers (ASHRAE) offers annual awards for exemplary HVAC designs, first on a "district-by-district" basis, and then nationally.

15 U.S. Department of Energy, "Building catalog: case studies of high performance buildings," accessed January 1, 2018, https://buildingdata.energy.gov/project/carnegie-institution-washington-global-ecology-center and Department of Global Ecology, Carnegie Institution for Science, accessed January 1, 2018, www.ehdd.com/work/ucstanford-department-of-global-ecology.

16 DualCool evaporatively precools both the condenser air and ventilation air, and as of 2017 had been installed on more than 2,000 rooftop units, mostly on "big-box" retail facilities in the U.S.
17 Solar Decathlon 2015, University of California, Davis, accessed January 1, 2018, www.solardecathlon.gov/2015/where-is-uc-davis-now.html.

11 Untapped potentials in Harold Hay's roof pond system for passive heating in cold climate regions

Daniel J. Overbey

Harold R. Hay did as much to advance high-performance building envelopes as any architect or engineer during the last half-century. Any text-book on architecture addressing "passive cooling" will reference Hay's roof pond system alongside courtyards, stack ventilation and others. Decades of white papers have chronicled the successes of test installations. A study developed for the US Department of Energy declared, "Well-designed roof pond systems can provide, without backup HVAC system, relatively even indoor temperatures (approximately 60 °F to 80 °F year-round) in climates with an outdoor temperature that ranges between 32 °F and 115 °F."[1] By such measures, the Hay's roof pond system is a success.

Yet, while it has been paid lip service in environmental systems classes for decades, one would find it difficult to meet any architect or engineer who has worked with a roof pond system or has seen one installed. There are myriad reasons for the lack of roof pond installations, but one seems the most obvious: the system is counterintuitive and defies some of the basic best practices of sound architectural design – namely, bulk water management. Architects and engineers are taught to shed water from atop a structure as efficiently as possible. Hay's roof pond system suggested quite the opposite. After all, water is the ideal thermal mass. It has the highest heat capacity of any naturally occurring substance and three times the thermal storage capacity of concrete at only half the weight of brick. To Hay, the proclivity to use water as a building material was a no-brainer. He was methodical, perseverant and brilliant – and always allowed data to guide him even if it led to solutions that flouted conventional materials, means and methods. Nowhere was this more apparent than with regard to his roof pond system, which he eventually trademarked as the "Skytherm" system for natural thermal control.

From movable insulation in India to water as thermal mass

Initially, however, what became the Skytherm system had nothing to do with water. Hay's discovery process began in the early 1950s during his tenure as an adviser to the Government of India where he was charged with improving building materials for low-cost housing. Hay began by studying indigenous materials and methods and compared them to "modern" (i.e., Western) materials and methods. He observed that traditional thatch roofs were being supplanted by asbestos-cement roofing assemblies and these non-traditional materials were having a negative impact on occupant comfort conditions. In response, he conducted a series of experiments in which he applied movable interior insulation to the asbestos-cement roofs and south masonry walls to control heat transfer throughout the day.

Hay's hypothesis proved correct. By manually moving the insulation, occupants could effectively manage heat migration through their building envelopes. He later determined that movable insulation could also serve to manage heat transfer during the winter months. As with the summer operation, the beneficial effect of the insulation was contingent on its mobility.[2]

Using water as a thermal mass

Following his work in India, Hay began adapting the concept of movable insulation to a water-based storage mass. He conducted experiments in Tempe, Arizona in 1966 and 1967 with 2-square-foot basins filled with 7 inches of water. Horizontal insulation covered the basins during the day, and the water was exposed to the sky at night. Results indicated that 6 inches of water provided adequate thermal storage for year-round air-conditioning.[3] As he once noted, "Water is the cheapest and most efficient heat storage material for buildings. Its fluid convection provides an outstanding advantage over the heat lag of solar materials."[4] Hay theorized that a combination of movable insulation atop a flat (slow-sloped) roof composed of water would yield thermally comfortable conditions even in the most challenging climate.

His experiments with water in Tempe caught the attention of the revered passive solar engineer, John I. Yellott. Thanks to Yellott's belief in the roof pond concept, Hay received an opportunity to test his theoretical system in a full-scale structure in the Sonoran Desert. Built in 1967, the 120-square-foot "Phoenix Prototype" was a rudimentary concrete block structure supporting a three-bay roof pond application complete with manually operated polyurethane movable insulation boards.[5]

Hay's innovation again proved fruitful. The prototype maintained an interior ambient air temperature between 70 °F and 80 °F during approximately 91% of the hours of the year under "normal" weather conditions in the hot-arid Phoenix climate. The interior ambient air temperatures were maintained in a range between 68 °F and 82 °F with daily temperature swings from 4 °F to 8 °F (with extremes of 2 °F and 12 °F).[6]

The rise of the roof pond

Spurred by the volatility of oil prices in the 1970s, the success of Hay and Yellott's roof pond research paved the way for Hay's marquee installation – a full-scale residence in Atascadero, California. The 1,192-square-foot "Atascadero House" was nearly ten times the size of the Phoenix prototype. The fully instrumented residence would test the capabilities of a 6,000-gallon 8.5-inch-deep roof pond system. Through its first full heating (1973–1974) and cooling (1974) seasons, the house required no auxiliary cooling/heating.[7]

Over the next ten years, the success of the Atascadero House would prompt nearly a dozen roof pond buildings across the contiguous United States. The US Department of Energy (DOE) took notice of Hay's innovative concept and commissioned a comprehensive study of every known roof pond installation of note.

Radical adaptation of the roof pond for cold climate regions

One of the more intriguing findings of the DOE report is that the roof pond system was capable of providing "both heating and cooling with no alteration of components."[8] Yet, virtually all of the projects were built in the hot-arid US Southwest where the heating requirement is not as challenging as in other parts of the country. Moreover, the system has some notable shortcomings with regard to its suitability in colder climate regions.

In the years following the Atascadero House, as interest in roof ponds reached its pinnacle, Hay conceived of an adaptation of his patented Skytherm system for northern regions of the US. Aware of the climatic differences, Hay understood the need for the system and its components to be enveloped by a pitched roof with south-facing skylights. Hay's "Skytherm North" system was essentially a roof pond to be installed within a building's thermal barrier in an unoccupied attic. The movable insulation also had to be relocated indoors to protect it from the elements.

Only one case study in the DOE report existed outside of the US Southwest and it was a Skytherm North application. A full-scale, 2,000-square-foot, two-story, single-family residence built in Inver Grove Heights outside of St. Paul, Minnesota provided a proof-of-concept for the north application of the roof pond (Fig. 11.1).

The "Skytherm North Residence," also called "St. Paul Residence," featured an 18-inch-deep roof pond that covered roughly half the floor area (the house also featured an atrium). In this application, a series of narrow water bags were mounted between the joists of the insulated, enclosed attic space. Because of the attic's special thermal function (and need for water-tightness), Hay coined it a "thermospace" in order to distinguish it from conventional attics. Beneath the water bags, a 22-gauge steel deck constituted the ceiling for the occupied spaces below. A series of white-painted 3-inch-thick rigid insulation panels were mounted to the top of the attic via barn door hinges, and were allowed to swing open. The house's two-story atrium fostered effective heat distribution (via radiation and convection) throughout the two-story space.[9] In addition to the roof pond, this house also contained a direct gain system by which the interior could collect

Figure 11.1 Above: Exterior view of the Skytherm North Residence near St.
Paul, Minnesota; Below: A view of the Skytherm North Residence's
thermospace and roof pond.

Source: Photos courtesy of University of Nevada, Las Vegas.

solar heat through south-facing glass. This suggests that Hay and the house's
designers understood that, although thermally stable, the living spaces may
struggle to effectively sequester solar heat gain when income is available
during the heating season in cold climates.

Skytherm North made several concessions to Hay's original invention. Its orientation-dependent condition required the thermospace's skylights to be positioned facing south. The movable insulation panels had to be automated, as they were not easily accessed – such a mechanism called into question the roof pond's categorization as a truly "passive" system.[10] Also, with regard to installed cost, certain economies of the system were lost as the configuration required two roofs: an uninsulated low-sloped roof for the water bags and a traditionally insulated pitched roof with skylights. For the St. Paul Residence, the passive solar features comprised 19% of the overall construction cost of the home.[11] Such considerations made the system a challenging sell for homeowners and small commercial facilities.

Regardless, the Skytherm North residence allegedly operated well. The thermal performance of the roof pond and use of the auxiliary heat system were not formally monitored. It was reported that the direct gain system contributed 6 °F to 8 °F to the temperature inside the house during the heating season. When the roof pond bags reached 90 °F, the upstairs inhabitable volume recorded a temperature of approximately 70 °F.[12] Considering such performance, the project offered a glimpse into the potential of Hay's roof pond in heating-dominated climates with considerable snow loads. Yet, since the prototype residence was constructed in 1979 (and subsequently demolished after the house was damaged years later), there was no record of another Skytherm North system being constructed until the Muncie Passive Solar Project.

The Muncie Passive Solar Project

For years, the Skytherm North Residence would be relegated as a largely theoretical passive heating strategy. In academic and professional circles, the system was largely unknown. The north application was all but missing from textbooks and academic accounts of Hay's roof pond system. However, by 2002, with generous support from the Evelyn and Harold Hay Fund, Ball State University moved forward with the Muncie Passive Solar Project (MPSP), a research initiative that provided the first account of a Skytherm North application with monitored performance data. Alfredo Fernández-González directed the MPSP through the Center for Energy Research/ Education/Service (CERES).[13]

Located in Muncie, Indiana, the MPSP consisted of side-by-side installations of test rooms or "cells" equipped with various passive solar heating systems. The project initially compared a well-insulated control cell without any source of heating to five passive solar test cells with otherwise identical construction: direct gain (DG), Trombe-wall (TW), water-wall (WW), sunspace (SS) and roof pond (RP). All the test cells had a floor area of 128 square feet (8 feet by 16 feet) with the smaller sides facing north and south. The MPSP test rooms were instrumented using a four-point grid in which each of the nodes had four sensors (two internal and two external) connected to data loggers.[14]

The roof pond used in this study was based on Hay's Skytherm North system. The water volume was contained within two permanently sealed clear polyethylene bags. The assembly was housed within a thermospace featuring a 43.6-square-foot skylight facing true (solar) south.[15] An insulated garage door that moved between the north and south slopes provided interior movable insulation. The garage door concept provided a convenient "off-the-shelf" solution to the need for a mechanically controlled movable insulation component on the interior side of the south-facing glazing. The movable insulation was automated and during the heating season it opened 45 minutes after sunrise and closed 45 minutes before sunset.[16]

The RP structure featured the highest thermal heat capacity among the five original passive solar test cells. As a result, it was the most thermally stable in terms of both time and heat distribution to the occupiable volume below. According to Fernández-González, the RP test cell also exhibited the best performance during the nighttime and extended periods of overcast sky conditions, which were quite frequent during the initial (2002–2003) heating season.[17]

Through the first heating season, Fernández-González also observed that though the RP test cell's performance during the daytime was not as good as the performance of the DG and WW test cells, the RP structure exhibited potential for performance improvements as it could be easily coupled with any of the other strategies.[18] The capability of being "coupled" with another passive solar heating system had been already identified by Hay in the St. Paul Residence.[19] After analyzing the results from the first heating season of the MPSP, Fernández-González disassembled the SS test cell and reconstructed it to feature both a roof pond and direct gain system. The resulting roof pond-direct gain (RP-DG) test cell offered a unique opportunity to monitor both strategies in isolation and in concert with each other (Fig. 11.2).[20]

The RP-DG test cell exhibited the highest thermal heat capacity of any test cell monitored at the MPSP test facility. The RP-DG cell featured a 12-inch roof pond assembly (the St. Paul Residence featured an 18-inch-deep roof pond). According to Fernández-González, the movable insulation was operated such that during the heating season it was opened 45 minutes after sunrise and closed 45 minutes before sunset. During the cooling season, this schedule was reversed.[21]

A validated methodology to predict the performance of Skytherm North

During the second heating season of the MPSP (2003–2004), the RP-DG test cell exhibited thermal performance superior to any other test cell.[22] However, the hybrid system was still largely unproven and defied conventional practice. Any potential for market uptake of Hay's Skytherm North system would necessarily hinge on a validated methodology and a suitable

Figure 11.2 The Muncie Passive Solar Project circa 2002. In this photo, the sunspace
(SS) test cell has been converted into a roof pond-direct gain (RP-DG)
hybrid test cell.

Source: Photo courtesy of Alfredo Fernández-González.

metric by which design teams may assess the potential heating performance
of the roof pond application.

Dr. J. Douglas Balcomb understood the need for practitioners to assess
the performance of passive solar strategies. His "solar savings fraction" (SSF)
has endured as a widely accepted metric used to assess the potential thermal
performance of buildings using passive solar heating strategies.[23] The SSF
may be defined as the extent to which a building's passive solar features
reduce a building's seasonal heating need versus a building devoid of any
passive solar component.[24] The standard procedure used to calculate the SSF
for a given design scenario is the "load collector ratio" (LCR) method. Such
a method was developed at the Los Alamos National Laboratory (LANL)
by Passive Solar Group Q-11, a team led by Dr. Balcomb.[25] Group Q-11
studied passive solar heating systems from 1977 through 1984 and found
that the primary factor that determines the performance of a passive solar
building in a particular climate is the ratio of the building heat loss load to
the area of the solar collector area – the load collector ratio. Though widely
accepted as the standard methodology for predicting passive solar heating
performance via the SSF metric, the LCR method has remained relatively
unchanged and unchallenged for nearly three decades.

However, by 2007 the author, working in concert with Fernández-
González, applied the LCR method to the MPSP and cross-referenced the
predicted SSF against the actual SSF of the continuously monitored passive
solar-heated test cells. Processing nearly two and half years of performance
data from the MPSP, the study assessed the aptness of the LCR method for

estimating the thermal performance of various passive solar heating strategies. The study revealed the difference between the LCR method's predicted SSF values and the MPSP test cells' actual SSF values had an average disparity of 4.7%. Ultimately, the study concluded that despite the test cells' deviation from the reference designs, the LCR method was acceptably accurate for predicting the cells' annual thermal performance at the schematic design phase.[26]

There is one caveat regarding the use of the LCR method. Dr. Balcomb and Los Alamos Group Q-11 studied the direct gain, Trombe-wall, water-wall and sunspace strategies.[27] However, they did not assess Hay's roof pond system, let alone the Skytherm North application.[28] While the LCR method has been leveraged by the architectural and engineering community over the past quarter-century to advance passive solar heating, the roof pond has always been at a major disadvantage. There has never been a basis to predict or compare Hay's roof pond system in terms of the SSF.

To address this, Fernández-González leveraged the RP and RP-DG test cell data from the MPSP to validate "RP_Performance," an interactive Microsoft® Excel™ spreadsheet that allows users to modify relevant parameters that influence the thermal performance of Skytherm North roof pond buildings. This design tool provides users with a ten-day temperature chart for a roof pond, energy conserving and reference building for any desired month. In addition, "RP_Performance" provides the SSF by comparing the roof pond against the reference building and the heating and cooling energy costs for the roof pond, energy conserving and reference building.[29] This platform unlocked new avenues for design teams to assess the relative performance of the Skytherm North system to other passive solar heating options.

The validation of the LCR method and "RP_Performance" marked unprecedented breakthroughs for a sustainable design community in need of a performance metric by which to compare passive solar strategies – including Hay's Skytherm North system – and to account for their potential impacts on a project's heating needs. The SSF could be leveraged for green building certification systems, as passive solar heating performance could be easily approximated during conceptual and schematic design studies using the SSF metric.

The superior performance of Skytherm North

The results of the MPSP suggested that a combination of passive heating (Skytherm North and direct gain) and cooling strategies (roof pond and night ventilation of mass), along with additional energy conservation efforts, could significantly reduce – and potentially eliminate – the energy requirement for space conditioning in residential buildings in Muncie and perhaps most of the northern US Midwest. The calculated SSF for the RP-DG test cell was approximately three times the SSF of the next best MPSP test cell.[30]

The promise of Hay's Skytherm North system to provide adequate heating was on full display in a predominantly cold climate region and tools to easily assess and implement such systems are now readily available.

In 2004, the author was involved in a collaborative design effort between the Greater Muncie, Indiana Habitat for Humanity affiliate (GMIHH) and Ball State University's Muncie Urban Design Studio (MUDS) to design eight innovative housing prototypes for potential future implementation. During the design process, four categories of design strategies/systems were identified for continued design development. One of them was "alternatives to conventional heating, ventilation, air-conditioning (HVAC) systems." The author worked in concert with CERES and leveraged RP_Performance to design an optimized passive solar-heated housing prototype exhibiting Hay's Skytherm North system coupled with a direct gain system (among other energy conservation measures) to achieve a predicted average SSF of 88.7%.[31] The roof pond prototype was formally introduced to the GMIHH and was even recognized by the American Solar Energy Society (ASES) for its innovative offerings. Yet despite the body of existing roof pond performance data and validated tools for proving its potential, the housing prototype suffered the same fate as those of Hay's roof pond concepts over the past five decades: the seemingly absurd notion that one would harbor a large amount of water within a roof structure, despite data suggesting that such a solution would exhibit superior thermal performance and energy cost savings.

The untapped genius of Harold R. Hay

In many ways, the story of Skytherm North epitomizes Hay's trials and successes as a visionary ahead of his time. Hay was attuned to the physics at play and allowed data to guide him to innovative solutions devoid of bias – unimpeded by conventional wisdom or standard practice. He came to recognize water as a superior thermal mass and understood its potential as a building material – no less a building material that is natural, widely available, cost-effective to access, stable, non-toxic, acoustically absorbent, shock-absorbent and offers fire-protection.

Perhaps soon the building design and construction industry will recognize the roof pond system for its immense untapped potential to make our housing stock more affordable to conditioning and more resilient in the face of increasingly severe climate changes. Perhaps then the design community will recognize Harold R. Hay for the genius that he truly was.

Notes

1 William P. Marlatt, Kathy A. Murray and Steven E. Squier, *Roof Pond Systems* (Canoga Park, CA: Energy Technology Engineering Center, 1984), 1.
2 Harold R. Hay, "Roofponds Ten Years Later: A Critique of the DOE Report by Rockwell International," paper published at the American Solar Energy Society SOLAR '85 Conference, Raleigh, North Carolina, October 1985.

3   Marlatt, Murray, Squier, *Roof Pond*, 2.

4   Harold R. Hay, "Natural Thermal Control for Innovative City Planning" (Solar Engineering, vol. H00467, 1989): 139–46.

5   Marlatt, Murray, Squier, *Roof Pond*, 2–4, and Harold R. Hay, "100% Natural Thermal Control – Plus," paper published at the Third International PLEA Conference, Mexico City, Mexico, August 1984.

6   Marlatt, Murray, Squier, *Roof Pond*, 2–5.

7   Ibid., 2–7.

8   Ibid., 1–9.

9   Hay, "100% Natural Thermal Control – Plus"; Marlatt, Murray, Squier, *Roof Pond*, 2–22.

10 Alfredo Fernández-González and Harold R. Hay, "Roofpond Building Design: Heating and Cooling Applications," paper published at the American Solar Energy Society SOLAR 2004 Conference, Portland, Oregon, July 2004.

11 Marlatt, Murray, Squier, *Roof Pond*, 2–23.

12 Ibid.

13 Alfredo Fernández-González, "Comfort and Thermal Performance of Passive Solar Test Rooms in Muncie, Indiana," paper published at the American Solar Energy Society SOLAR 2004 Conference, Portland, Oregon, July 2004.

14 Ibid.

15 Daniel J. Overbey, "Validation of the Load Collector Ratio (LCR) Method and Solar Load Ratio (SLR) Method for Predicting the Thermal Performance from Five Passive Solar Test Rooms Using Measured Data," paper published at the American Solar Energy Society SOLAR 2008 Conference, San Diego, California, July 2008.

16 Fernández-González, "Comfort and Thermal Performance."

17 Ibid.

18 Ibid.

19 Marlatt, Murray, Squier, *Roof Pond*, 2–23.

20 Fernández-González, "Comfort and Thermal Performance"; and "Defining the Optimum Dimensions of Test-Cells to Research Thermal Comfort in Passive Solar Buildings: A Direct Comparison Study," paper published at the American Solar Energy Society SOLAR 2003 Conference, Austin, Texas, July 2003.

21 Fernández-González, "Comfort and Thermal Performance."

22 Overbey, "Validation of the Load Collector Ratio (LCR) Method."

23 Fuller Moore, *Environmental Control Systems: Heating, Cooling, Lighting* (New York: McGraw-Hill, 1993), 115.

24 Walter T. Grondzik and Alison G. Kwok, *Mechanical and Electrical Equipment for Buildings* (Hoboken, NJ: John Wiley & Sons, Inc., 2015), 301.

25 Douglas J Balcomb, Robert W. Jones, Robert D. McFarland and William O. Wray, *Passive Solar Heating Analysis: A Design Manual* (Atlanta, GA: American Society of Heating, Refrigerating and Air-Conditioning Engineers, 1984).

26 Daniel J. Overbey, "Validation of the Load Collector Ratio (LCR) Method for Predicting the Thermal Performance from Five Passive Solar Test Rooms Using Measured Data," M.Arch Thesis, University of Nevada, Las Vegas, 2007.

27 Balcomb, Jones, Wray, *Passive Solar Heating Analysis: A Design Manual.*

28 In personal conversations with the author, Hay suggested that Balcomb's exclusion of the roof pond was motivated by personal differences. However, the author sees no evidence of this and believes there are three primary reasons why Group

Q-11 did not consider roof ponds in their studies at Los Alamos: 1) at that point in their research, the roof pond was largely considered a passive cooling system; 2) the original southwest roof pond archetype uses the low-sloped roof as the solar collector area whereas all of the other passive solar heating systems studied by Balcomb and Group Q-11 used the south-oriented face of a structure; and 3) Hay had a patent on the roof pond under the "Skytherm" trademark, which was likely a deterrent due to said personal differences.

29 Fernández-González, "Comfort and Thermal Performance."

30 Alfredo Fernández-González and Daniel J. Overbey, "Heating and Cooling Performance of a Roofpond-Direct Gain Test Cell," paper published at the American Solar Energy Society SOLAR 2008 Conference, San Diego, California, July 2008.

31 Daniel J. Overbey, "A Roofpond System for Natural Air-Conditioning in a Habitat for Humanity Home in Muncie, Indiana," paper published at the American Solar Energy Society SOLAR 2004 Conference, Portland, Oregon, July 2004.

Part III

Necessity and pleasure

12 Building experience

Dale Clifford

My recent stay at a Ramada Inn in the Midwest began in a lobby with no natural light, which led to a confusing series of sheet-rock lined, carpeted, double-loaded corridors that smelled of perfumed cleaning fluid. Finally, the wood-grained formica door opened to a polyester-carpeted "large" room with vinyl wallpaper and an acoustic-panel ceiling. Though the smell was stifling; the anodized aluminum window was not operable. Synthetic (and sometimes toxic) interiors of typical lodgings scattered in polluted landscapes characterize today's throw-away environment.

Steven Holl[1]

This is no walk in the woods. The scenario above has likely been felt by all of us at one time or another, and depending on where and how we live, with unfortunate frequency. Steven Holl describes our cultured ability to disregard our environment by desensitizing ourselves to stimuli that affront the senses, an ability that leads to environmental indifference. He portrays our estrangement from material origins, our often-toxic relationship with buildings that we cannot operate and the resultant condition of our detached relationship to the environment. One can imagine entering the scenario above, shades drawn, television and air-conditioning on, a temporal and noxious safe-house from a perhaps more contaminated and less-cared-for environment outside. It is easy to blame this condition on technology and contemporary profit-driven construction practices, but the tone of this chapter is neither angry nor nostalgic; it attempts to rethink the role of materials and technology and their ability to reconnect us to the dynamics of the environment.

The complexity of climate is a dynamic condition that we have evolved to read and act upon, yet most buildings are designed for stasis and to maintain consistent comfort levels for their occupants. When deviations in comfort levels are sensed or perceived, energy is input into the system to heat, cool, humidify or dehumidify in order to maintain these levels. Advances in building technology have enabled narrower bands of comfort and with this advancement we have progressively separated ourselves from the environment, insulating ourselves from change. Though buildings are able to maintain comfort levels, they have become less adept at satisfying our physical and psychological well-being. The intent of this chapter is to construct a narrative where buildings are made dynamic, engage the senses and (re)sensitize occupants by situating them in closer context with environmental fluctuations. This thinking is partially drawn from Icelandic-Danish artist, Olafur Eliasson, who is a fabricator of autonomous and anthropomorphic machines that sense and interact with wind patterns. Eliasson sustains that "when surroundings are thought of as stable, we tend to lose a feeling of responsibility for the environments in which we move," which is precisely what often happens when we think of buildings as stable.[2]

A more dynamic response to local conditions resists the homogenization of globalized building practices and suggests, as in the past, that an environmentally and technologically adept architecture reveals local nuances that can appeal to the imagination and reconnect us emotively to the qualities of a place. In his book "Genus Loci," whose title refers to the "spirit of place," the Norwegian architect and theorist Christian Norberg-Schulz understood this as an "existential foothold," a way of understanding our relationship to the world that is dependent upon emotive and visceral experience, and cannot be gained through scientific understanding alone.[3] It is speculated that, as we spend most of our time in buildings, if our built environment were made dynamic and more able to respond to environmental nuance, then this would reengage us, emotively, viscerally and instinctively, with the natural world.

Responsive materials and systems

Dynamic or responsive architectural design varies in its underlying strategies, from the computational and electronic to more passive material-based systems that are reactive to environmental stimuli.[4] This chapter suggests an approach to building design that applies dynamic materials that exhibit behavioral change in response to environmental fluctuations; specifically, the prospect for materials to contribute quantitatively and qualitatively to the performance of buildings. These dynamic materials are part of an emerging class of programmable matter that can be tailored to trigger or "switch" in response to specific environmental stimuli such as light, temperature or humidity. This chapter discusses current projects, developed in collaboration with professional partners and with students at Cal Poly, San Luis Obispo, that contribute to lowering building energy consumption and address the waning physical connection of building to place, and to an inhabitant's emotive connection to nature. This research has become a platform to better understand the role of new materials in the buildings we construct and how to leverage these properties to restructure our relationship with the dynamics of the environment.

Situating

Buildings have long been designed to adapt to environmental conditions. Until recently, nearly all construction revealed directness to geography and climate, and as a result, contributed to cultural richness. Early examples of building technology, whether shutters, sunscreens or operable windows, are examples of adaptive components that integrated the built environment, the natural environment and the built and natural environment. Their combined performance with aesthetics allowed for an experiential understanding of context as one manipulated the forces of wind, heat and light to adjust the quality of interior spaces. Our understanding of, and interaction with, these simple passive systems lowered reliance on heating and cooling systems, and experientially conjoined a building to both its context and inhabitants.

In recent decades, this experiential understanding has diminished with the progressive optimization of building mechanical systems, designed to deliver thermal and optical (sensorial) uniformity. The preference toward engineering artificial environments has simultaneously compromised our relationship with the dynamics of the natural environment, making us perhaps more desensitized to our surroundings than ever.[5] In times when environmental activism constitutes a very present social and political force, our lack of environmental understanding seems a significant paradox. For instance, in contemporary office buildings there has been a shift from manual operability of heat, light and air, in favor of sealed building envelopes with interior spaces regulated by centralized, yet sensually distant sources.

Beyond the negative physical effects of sick-building syndrome, in which occupants complain of acute physical illness and "report relief soon after leaving the building," the strategy of optimized central control has isolated the inhabitant from the dynamics of natural environments.[6] In response, there is a branch of research that seeks to apply the dynamic qualities of responsive materials to enable buildings to passively self-regulate and tune themselves to environmental changes.[7] This research asserts that the environment is not the backdrop for human activity, but a ubiquitous foreground through which we are continually made present and aware. In terms of architecture, these are buildings that filter and intensify one's relationship with the environment by adapting in real-time to the changing conditions of light, temperature, humidity and other environmental fluctuations. The goal of this project is to dig deeper, cross disciplinary boundaries and envision ways to disrupt the continued optimization of mechanical systems by searching for innovative methods to resituate our relationship with buildings and, by extension, our relationship with nature.

Programmable materials

Materials have long shaped the way designers think and influence the artificial environments we construct. Recent advances in materials science have enabled designers to conceive of a built environment that is homeo-static – the biological condition where organisms maintain internal sta-bility through the continuous exchange of matter and energy with the local environment.[8] Together, architects and material scientists are questioning the role of building components and systems in contemporary construction, specifically the tradition of building with static materials and the opportun-ities afforded by dynamic, or smart materials. The latter embed sensing and actuation within their internal structure and efforts are being made to gain control over the dynamic characteristics of smartness, ushering an emergent field of programmable matter. These materials have trigger points, at which they exhibit variable characteristics, effectively conjoining matter and com-putation. For instance, a shape memory alloy can be programmed to assume a specific preset shape at a predetermined temperature. These materials have the prospect to give the built environment a durable and reliable capacity for self-regulation.

Phase-change materials (PCMs) are the target of this study as their respon-sive properties can be tailored to respond to temperature and they have the prospect to contribute quantitatively and qualitatively to building perform-ance. They are also low cost and potentially open source, meaning that a variety of materials may be used that exhibit phase-change characteristics, such as coconut oil and honey. These are less effective than engineered materials but still highly effective at thermal storage, and it is likely that a simple method of programming these materials exists. Design equity can take many forms, and in the current context of the widening gap between the elite and the majority of the population, this project searches for ways to bring interesting, interactive and low-cost building technology to a wide section of the populous.

Phase-change background

Water, the PCM we are most familiar with, and that was central in Harold Hay's roof pond system, crystalizes at 0 °C, taking on a more ordered internal structure. Such ordering or crystal building requires energy and absorbs heat from the surrounding environment. Conversely, when solid water melts, it assumes a less energetic state, releasing stored energy to the environ-ment. PCMs (organic fatty acids like coconut oil, paraffin and salt-based solutions) operate on the same principle, though the melt/freeze point can be programmed. A common use for PCMs is the linings of take-out pizza bags. Stored on top of the pizza oven, the material absorbs heat and once removed releases heat to the pizza on that long ride. When programmed to freeze/melt at ambient room temperatures PCM is extremely effective at stabilizing temperature swings. It is this property that has great potential to reduce the immense amounts of energy buildings require to maintain temperature.

Some PCMs are so effective at heat retention, they have a thermal storage capacity an order of magnitude higher than concrete when undergoing phase transition. For example, a one-inch-thick panel of PCM that could switch from opaque to transparent has the thermal storage equivalency of ten inches of concrete. Imagine a cave that maintains a constant temperature as a result of massive walls. Now imagine that the walls of the cave would sometimes be opaque (late evening/early morning), sometimes translucent (afternoon/evening) and sometimes transparent (late afternoon/early evening).

Adaptive architecture

Many fields are shifting from the industrial paradigm of mechanics to the softer and more pliant approach of programmable materials. Robotics, an early adopter of this shift with the fledgling field of "soft" robotics, modeled on insects, uses flexible materials such as shape memory alloys, silicone and pneumatics, rather than gears and motors, to achieve silent actuation and high dexterity. A parallel shift is underway in the field of architecture where responsive technologies vary in underlying strategies, from the computational and electronic to more passive material-based systems that are reactive to environmental stimuli. If we become adept at working with materials that change their properties in response to light, temperature and other stimuli, then we can adopt a more pliant approach to designing buildings with materially responsive operative filters, rather than the common practice of building barriers between interior and exterior. Adopting a more interactive model of design that integrates advances in materials science offers an alternative for displacing reductionist and mechanical views of nature.

The science of building technology is currently driven by the necessity to reduce energy consumption. However, the reduction of architecture to just resources and uses poses some of the same dangers that the reduction of architecture to mechanical systems created. Instead, the project that follows is a shift from emphasis on form-making toward an ethic of building performance. The project is an effort to make PCMs more programmable, sensorial, lower in cost and more energy effective for building applications. The intent is not only to lower reliance on mechanical conditioning, but is meant to be visually compelling and appeal to the imagination. The PCM Tile project passively stores and releases thermal energy while exhibiting behavioral change in response to environmental temperature change.

Phase-change tiles

The Tile Project was driven by an initial observation when playing with coconut oil, which has a freeze/melt point slightly above room temperature. Below this temperature, the oil solidifies, making interesting crystallization patterns while absorbing thermal energy from the surrounding environment.

This observation led to an interest in the correlation of thermal performance and visual patterning, and more specifically in the psychological effect to the phenomenal nuances of change. The proposition is that we make better choices regarding thermal comfort (turning up the thermostat) if we are aware that the building itself is dynamic and at "work" applying material properties to passively respond to environmental fluctuation. These ideas draw from Holl's understanding that "as a catalyst for change, architecture's ability to shape our daily experiences in material and detail is subtle yet powerful. When sensory experience is intensified, psychological dimensions are engaged." This thought was also in line with Hay's early vision that engaging with passive energy design would contribute to the making of better societies.

The phase-change tiles are a set of design prototypes that explore the high thermal storage density and visual nature of these materials. The current design extracts the material from its normative location within a wall and positions it as a separate element for application on building interiors (Fig. 12.1). An early application of the tiles was designed for Bohlin Cywinski Jackson Architects to help meet the net-zero energy petal and education petal of the Living Building Challenge for the Frick Environmental Center in Pittsburgh, PA and contribute to the center's educational mission to convey sustainable principles to the public. Our collaborative design team, including architects and mechanical engineers, proposed novel packaging systems that reveal the crystal growth patterns during transition while exposing more PCM to the air, making the material highly effective at thermal transmission and visually conveying the buildings' dynamic response to temperature change (Fig. 12.2). These two attributes fit the sustainable and educational mission of the Environmental Center. Placed on the interior of a south-facing window system, the PCM tile was designed to effectively absorb and store heat from the sun in the afternoon then release heat in the evening when temperatures drop below 76 °F. In effect, the tiles provide thermal comfort by adding substantial dynamic mass to the building.

Prototypes and design process

Physical modeling has been essential throughout this project due to the reactive material qualities. Early on we understood that the depth of the PCM container was critical to allow the visual crystallization patterns to be made evident. Early prototypes were made from cast glass and cut glass, but due to the high cost and time investment, our team moved to glued layers of gasketed acrylic, a technology used to adhere rear-view mirrors to substrates that was borrowed from the automotive industry. Prototypes were always built at full-scale and were invaluable as visual mock-ups for the design team and potential clients. Beyond the collaboration with professional partners,

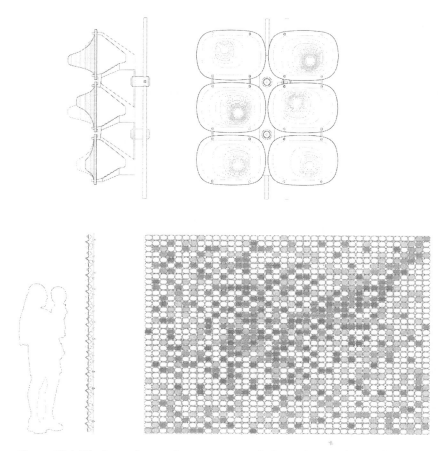

Figure 12.1 The lower image shows an array of phase-change tiles attached to the interior of a curtain wall system. Tiles are filled with phase-change material with varying temperature set points, evident in the patterns made by the difference in translucency of the individual tiles. The upper images show a phase-change material vessel and mounting system. The vessels vary in volume and shape, offsetting the time it takes for the material to freeze/melt and varying the translucency of each vessel.

Source: Drawings by Cal Poly students in author's class.

the PCM tiles were further developed in the Cal Poly Materials Innovation Lab, a course sequence that searches for new applications of both traditional and emergent materials.[9] Students worked in teams to refine individual tiles, then arrayed these into larger combinations. Because of the lab setting, we were able to uncover a high degree of variation in patterning and geometry. Taken singularly, the tiles are simple, though as a field, a variety of

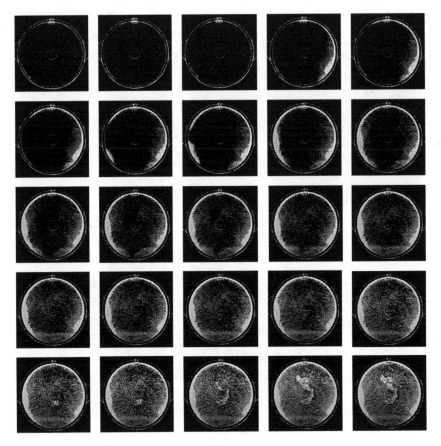

Figure 12.2 Matrix of phase-change tiles as they change from near optically clear to opaque as the material freezes. Temperature is decreasing (74 °F–70 °F) from upper left to lower right.

Source: Image by author.

visual conditions occur and patterns emerge (Fig. 12.3). This lateral investigation has opened new avenues that are leading to further partnerships with professional practice and searches for low-cost and compelling energy technologies.

On mass and transparency

Thermal mass has long been used to stabilize temperature in buildings. In 1881 Edward Morse developed and patented a standardized technology that later became known as the "Trombe" wall system. And in 1967 Hay patented his Skytherm system which used water as thermal mass. As contemporary buildings

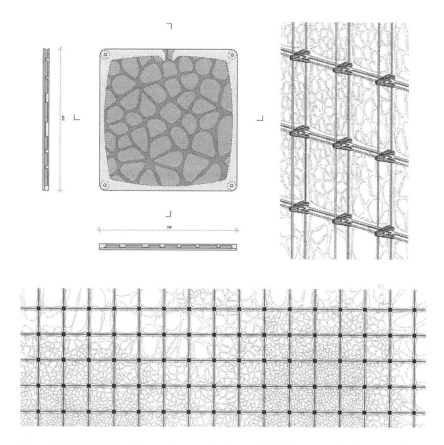

Figure 12.3 Individual phase-change tile (upper left) shown with deeper pockets in light gray that hold more phase-change material than the surrounding dark-gray channels. Varying thickness within a single tile varies the freeze/melt rate and the degree of translucency over time. When arranged into a larger assembly, the wall system operates as a coordinated temperature-responsive visual field and thermal energy storage system.

Source: Drawings by Cal Poly students in author's class.

shed their mass and trend toward lightness and transparency, air-conditioning systems are the primary means of maintaining thermal comfort within commercial buildings. The PCM tiles are an advancement of the mentioned inventions that operated using thermal mass systems, yet are far more effective at thermal storage during phase transition than concrete or water, making for a "light" and sometimes-transparent mass. Early studies show that if PCM tiles were innovatively designed and integrated into buildings as proposed, heating and cooling loads could be substantially reduced or eliminated in many commercial building types in climatic regions like Los Angeles and Shanghai.[10]

Conclusion

American author, marine biologist and conservationist Rachel Carson stated, "the control of nature is a phrase conceived in arrogance, born of the Neanderthal age of biology and philosophy, when it was supposed that nature exists for the convenience of man."[11] Carson went further and identified the complex, interactive and interdependent network of life and made clear that human action disproportionately impacts the network. The control of nature has been a fundamental underpinning for architecture and engineering and these disciplines might well be added to Carson's list. We are now entering a more "responsive" age of architecture, biology and engineering, and the design disciplines are engaging the sciences to forward a more synthetic approach to the places we build and those we inhabit. It is suggested here that this approach will enable buildings to sense environmental changes and respond in real time to optimized energy usage.

In tandem to energy efficiency, an equally important aspect of this research is to advance the prospect of building technology to be dynamic, sensual and appeal to the imagination, thereby more viscerally connecting occupants to environmental changes and modifying our behavior in regards to consumption. A position is taken that the directive of modern sustainable building technology is not solely human comfort but a nuanced understanding of our relationship to and with the environment.

Notes

1 Stephen Holl, *Parallax* (New York: Princeton Architectural Press, 2000), 71.
2 Olfur Elliasson (ed.) and Emily Abruzzo, *Models* (New York: Princeton Architectural Press, 2007), 19.
3 Christian Norberg-Schulz, *Genius Loci: Towards a Phenomenology of Architecture* (New York: Rizzoli, 1980).
4 Frederick Kiesler, "On Correalism and Biotechnique: A Definition and Test of a New Approach to Building Design," *The Architectural Record* (September 1939): 60–75; William Braham, "Biotechniques: Remarks on the Intensity of Conditioning," in *Performative Architecture*, eds. Ali Malkawi and Branko Kolarevic (London: Spon Press, 2004), 55–70.
5 Reyner Banham, *The Architecture of the Well-Tempered Environment* (Chicago, IL: University of Chicago Press, 1984), 171–194.
6 Indoor Air Facts No. 4 Sick building syndrome, accessed July 2018, www.epa.gov/indoor-air-quality-iaq/indoor-air-facts-no-4-sick-building-syndrome.
7 Many collaborative and experimental projects using dynamic materials to improve building energy performance are being supported by The Department of Energy and The National Science Foundation.
8 While all materials are effected by stimuli such as heat or moisture, dynamic materials significantly alter their properties and behavior in the presence of stimuli.

9 The Materials Innovation Lab course was taught collaboratively with Prof. Jeff Ponitz at Cal Poly, San Luis Obispo.

10 Conversations with Prof. Shi-chune Yao, Mechanical Engineering Dept., Carnegie Mellon University.

11 Rachel Carson, Lois Darling and Louis Darling, *Silent Spring* (Boston, MA: Houghton Mifflin, 1962), 261.

13 Thermal landscaping of buildings
Climate-proofing design

Susan Roaf

All around us buildings are failing for two main environmental design-related reasons:

a) They were built in the wrong place (too hot, cold, wet or windy).
b) They are wrongly built to withstand current and/or future climates.

Hurricanes Irma, Jose and Maria in 2017 proved once again how much climate-conscious design matters. In our *Ecohouse* design guide we describe different ways in which good design might be used to combat the impacts of extreme rain and winds and we shared two case studies on how to design to survive hurricanes with examples in Key West, Florida and on Saint Maarten in the Antilles in the Caribbean.[1] While both "ecohome" examples survived well, thousands of others did not as a large proportion of buildings in the path of those events failed. Wind damage is easy to see and assess. The impacts of excessive heat or cold are far less visible but nonetheless dangerous to us and to future generations. The architectural supertanker of "Business as Usual" is visibly and invisibly failing us now. It often works along the lines of "if everyone else is doing it, it can't be wrong."

But how does architecture evolve? Over the last ten thousand years humans have developed unique local architectures that have advanced in local climates. From indigenous materials to skills involving furnishings, fittings and clothing, people ensured they could remain comfortable in different temperatures. Climatic design in vernacular buildings starts with settlement, as structures were molded by landforms, solar and wind systems.

In antique lands, buildings and lifestyles co-evolved over millennia, forming the vernacular archetypes that grew organically together with human inventiveness. Architect James Marston Fitch highlights the ingenuity of late eighteenth-century American builders who soon developed what he characterized as four main house archetypes:[2]

1. The compact, centralized, close-clipped house of New England: wood or masonry homes with small windows and rooms, low ceilings with

modest heating volumes to endure long hard winters and relatively cool summers in.

2. Plantation houses of the Middle Seaboard colonies: Palladian in plan with high ceilings, larger windows, porches and porticoes.
3. The stilted, airy pavilions of the Louisiana French: under parasol roofs and perimeter galleries and balconies to shade the timber or masonry house from sun and rain, designed with large windows, high ceilings and central halls to encourage ventilation.
4. The inward-turning, patio-centered, mud masonry hacienda of the Southwest: thick walls, few windows toward the outer world with larger openings toward the shaded patios and courts, tempering extreme diurnal temperature ranges with mass indoors.

As an example, the New England close-clipped house would be unbearable in the summer heat and humidity of Louisiana where comfort depended on air movement over the skin and the deep shade of porches. By the mid-nineteenth century every American region and community had evolved its own locally appropriate building archetype for homes and public buildings. Archetypes informed new design skillsets and building markets. They created new social rules shaped not only by evolving building forms but by cultural constraints and moral codes that influenced everyday activity regimes.

Recent work by Fergus Nicol demonstrates that people around the world adapt to different local climates and consequently are comfortable in a huge range of different temperatures at home.[3] Importantly his studies show that there is a universally shared "sweet zone" for indoor climates from the UK to Saudi Arabia and Japan, ranging in winter between around 10 °C and 25 °C (50 °F–77 °F) and in summer from around 20 °C to 35 °C (68 °F–95 °F). This zone can be accommodated universally in diverse cultures by choice of dress, behaviors, building types and local technologies. Nicol's research demonstrates that for indoor temperatures of between 10 °C and 35 °C (50 °F–95 °F) locally adapted populations can find comfort in different ways. Such a work gives a robust indication of the thresholds above and below which adapted populations will be challenged in terms of their health and comfort. These credible thresholds are key in understanding what constitutes acceptable or dangerous conditions, as well as acceptable indoor temperatures.

The core body temperature of our species has changed little over millennia, hovering around 37 °C (98.5 °F) and supported by a complex system of thermo-regulatory processes evolved to manage and maintain thermal equilibrium. Metabolic energy fuels the engines of those systems and the further away from our core temperature the micro-climates around us become, the more energy is required to keep the core at 37 °C. There is also a physiological sweet zone in the human thermal system, a band of temperatures in which the body needs to take little or no action to make itself warmer or cooler while still maintaining core temperatures. This is termed the "Thermoneutral Zone" (TNZ). Each species has its own TNZ and empirical studies over the past few decades indicate that for a generic nude, resting adult the TNZ ranges from around 28 °C to 32 °C, as indicated in Figure 13.1.[4] Of course there are huge differences between the TNZs of different individuals at any time in any place, based on a myriad of factors, be they physical (e.g., relative humidity, air speed, weather, climate and the radiant, convective and conductive components of the environment); physiological (the morphology of the body, body composition, sex and physical activity); behavioral (clothing, movement, temporal adaptive adjustments etc.); and psychological (attitudes, expectations and habits). People simply adapt to those conditions they occupy and if they are uncomfortable they change their clothing, activities or local environments to make themselves more comfortable.[5]

Above upper skin temperature (around 35 °C or 95 °F) sweating is the key cooling mechanism for the body. It soon becomes socially unacceptable to undress further so people open windows or turn on fans to increase wind speeds locally and heat loss from the skin. Some people in very hot climates wear looser clothes to create cooler micro-climates next to the skin. When local climates are either much hotter or colder than locally acceptable temperature ranges, we rely on buildings to keep us safe. At both extremes, aggravated thermal stress from heat or cold can cause death.

As the world becomes warmer, the history of building evolution is challenged by thermal extremes that are severely affecting entire populations. Does this matter to us?

In less than a century, most US homes acquired air-conditioning. This trend keeps spreading around the world and has resulted in the ability of non-adapted populations to occupy some of the most inhospitable climates in the world, the Gulf region being a prime example.

Willis Carrier, father of American air-conditioning, framed the dream of the "air-conditioned life":

> at any time of year: the average business man will rise, pleasantly refreshed, having slept in an air-conditioned room, he will travel in an air-conditioned train, and toil in an air-conditioned office, store or factory – and dine in an air-conditioned restaurant. In fact, the only time he will know anything about the arctic blasts will be when he exposes himself to the natural discomforts outdoors.[6]

The US air-conditioning industry dreamed up comfort zones that would require us to live in temperatures between 20 °C and 26 °C (68 °F–78 °F), thus creating a huge demand for machines and a monumental energy burden to maintain such temperatures indoors in poorly designed and constructed buildings. Unfortunately, the more one spends on machines, the less one can spend on buildings. Many architects have been covertly shepherded into

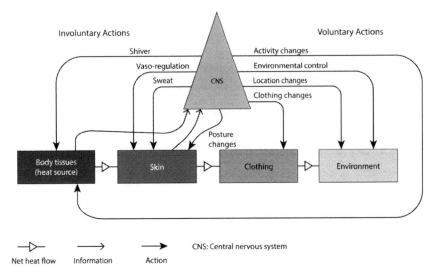

Figure 13.1 The classic diagram of the thermo-regulatory system showing physiological and behavioral feedback loops in conditions of subjective warmth with the net heat flow pathways from the body core to the environment.

Source: Michael Humphreys, Fergus Nicol and Susan Roaf, *Adaptive Thermal Comfort: Foundations and Analysis* (London: Earthscan/Routledge 2015), Drawn by Ken Butcher at CIBSE.

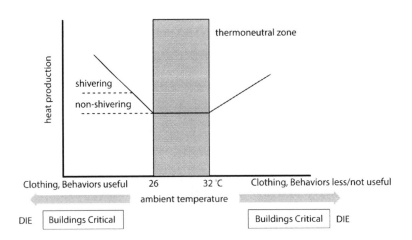

Figure 13.2 Diagram showing that thermal conditions are coped with in different ways. Below the thermoneutral zone people usually start involuntarily shivering, putting on more clothes and being more active. Diagram by author.

creating cheaper, over-serviced, short-life buildings that are fundamentally programmed to fail in four major ways:

1. **Energy dependence** on imported electricity to drive heating, cooling and communications systems and services, often causing buildings to fail during power outages. In the wake of many recent hurricanes and heat waves across the world, electricity outages have lasted from a few hours to weeks. Extraordinarily, many modern buildings lack opening windows to provide essential fresh air and cooling breezes so that during power outages their indoor air can rapidly become too hot/ fetid to safely occupy, as was the case in numerous buildings during Hurricane Sandy in New York.[7]

2. **Over-glazed buildings** often cause chronic over-heating or cooling, resulting in either huge electricity bills to solve the problem mechanically or alternatively extreme occupant discomfort. In 2016 HKS Inc. and Skidmore, Owings & Merrill settled out of court for millions of dollars in a suit brought by the Beacon Residential Community Association. Some of the units in a 595-unit luxury condominium complex in San Francisco were over-glazed with insufficient opening windows to the extent that they became unoccupiable. The suit deemed that the architects were responsible and had the obligation to provide fit-for-purpose accommodation both now and for the future.[8]

3. **Flimsy construction and poor climatic design** result in widespread damage during extreme weather events across the globe. The modern trend to build with ever-cheaper timber and steel-frame systems has led to a growing incidence of wind damage, even in relatively tightly regulated Scotland where high winds are common. In the 1993 Braer storm, the most intense extratropical cyclone ever recorded over the northern Atlantic Ocean (913mb pressure), Scotland did not lose a single roof. Currently, hundreds of modern rooves are being lost each year in far lower wind speeds.

4. **High-energy lifestyles** are expensive. Buildings designed to rely on mechanical systems to maintain comfortable conditions indoors rely also on the ability of their occupants to pay for the energy to run those machines. Developer-driven construction aims to minimize first costs and, by the time the building is occupied, architects and developers have already been paid and seldom return to assess the success of their designs. Unemployment, zero-hour contracts, lower wages and the phenomenon of the "disappearing middle classes," whose buying power diminishes with static wages and rising living costs, drive rising levels of fuel poverty within most socio-economic classes.

In opposition to these trends, passive energy design has provided a long-standing, lower-impact, viable and more ethical alternative approach to design. Although architectural activism has been historically driven by a "nudge process," its place in resisting unsustainable developments with new ways of approaching design cannot be undervalued. Harold Hay's work is often recognized as an act of activism against the use of air-conditioning in residential constructions. Hay lived through the Great Depression and his work was inculcated with a deep belief that more can be done with less. As he used to say, "you don't need electricity to cool! You don't need an air conditioner! You do it with the sky."[9] In 1967, he scraped together the money to build a one-room test home for his Skytherm system in Phoenix that harvested from and also lost heat to the sky as required to produce comfort in conjunction with thermal storage indoors. Hay finally built a full-scale model in Atascadero, California in 1973. Two years later, Hay's Skytherm house was recognized by the American Revolution Bicentennial Commission as one of the country's 200 most promising inventions. In this actively passive system he created a robust, natural energy-driven, low-cost heating and cooling system on the roof. The earliest version operated without electricity, making it a purely passive solar technology able to work even when the grid failed. It was a revolutionary way of thinking about heat flows around buildings and effective harvesting from solar gain. Somehow, those solar dreams failed to migrate into the US mass housing markets.

Yet, the possibility for a design revolution that can have lasting traction in those markets remains necessary. It is proposed here that such change should continue to build upon Hay's understanding of solar buildings as dynamic thermal systems. This idea, indeed, is not a new one as it can be found in ancient and diverse cultures. In addition, it should heighten adaptive comfort opportunities by inhabiting the actively passive house with active dwellers. The basis for such an idea, in light of today's world, should consider the following ABC of resilient design:

1. **Adaptation** will involve building occupants changing locations within buildings to harvest the heat and coolth flows, cycles and stores within buildings, particularly during extreme weather events. Thus, changing location becomes an identified opportunity in the well-known adaptive comfort feedback systems diagram (Fig. 13.1).
2. **Buildings** should be thermally landscaped to provide a range of different passive indoor micro-climates resulting from those flows that can be exploited by occupants as and when required.
3. **Climates** will become more extreme and power outages will become common, making it important to design climate refuges – climate-safe spaces – in most buildings in which to shelter from unsafe temperatures for short or longer periods.

The thermal landscaping of buildings

Indigenous people often moved seasonally in search of safe and acceptable micro-climates. Nomadic populations evolved a large variety of tent forms and constructions that were occupied by tribes from the frozen tundra regions of the Arctic to the roasting deserts of Africa, the Saudi peninsular and Asia. By using seasonal migration patterns, they occupied richer pasture lands and avoided those with thermal extremes of winters or summers. An extraordinary range of opportunities for harvesting heat and coolth from within and around one building can be explored and developed today by re-considering from the past:

1. **Earth coupling:** As early human populations moved further north and south into colder and hotter climates, they learnt to protect themselves from increasingly hostile climates by making clothes from skins, bark and feathers and constructing robust shelters. Neolithic man favored safe, warm/cool caves for homes and by the end of the last ice age (c.1200 years ago) people around the world were also living in the "First International Style" of building: the semi-underground structures built of timber, rock, stone or mud with stone, timber or turf roofs over them. In some areas today, such homes dating from 10,000–5,000 BC are still used. These ultimate super-insulated, semi-buried homes were designed to ensure inside comfort by thermally coupling indoor micro-climates to the dependable, stable earth temperatures.

2. **Sky coupling:** While digging deep into the earth gives stable temperature, extending structures into the sky couples them to the rapidly changing weather conditions around a building. Air around buildings can be harvested by simply inhabiting the various parts of the dwelling at the right time of the day. Manifest in Greek, Roman, Indian and Chinese palaces, such visible and invisible networks of airways and heat and coolth paths characterized the internal comfort of rooms. Hay's Skytherm system was a relatively sophisticated, low-energy, water engine for managing sky-coupled heat flows thermo-dynamically, but it required considerable manual management to optimize its operation unlike some of the more traditional systems like courtyards, wind-catchers and others.

3. **Sun coupling:** From earliest times, and in most cultures from Saxon England to the Puebloan tribes of America, solaria were designed to provide vital heat in cold weather. A well-made building with one warm solarium can provide some comfort even in the coldest winters.

4. **Ransom zones:** In extremely hot or cold weather, whole areas of buildings can be designed to be abandoned as thermal ransom zones to enable occupants to use them as thermal buffer zones. In traditional Baghdadi homes, the top floors are not used in the heat of summer but protect the floors below from the grueling solar gain. Inversely, in colder climates people would traditionally congregate in the warmest spaces, quite often around a living room or kitchen fire, abandoning upper floors until they were negotiated with the help of hot water bottles and warm bedding. Buildings could now be designed with ransom zones, including west-facing rooms or the top floors to be abandoned in

heatwaves. Even in simple terraced homes, designers are now getting interested in exploring the implications of the cool and the warm sides of the house for seasonal inhabitation and planning for different weather conditions.[10] Could not a roof pond system also be considered as a ransom zone to protect those below from weather extremes using its managed thermal states?

Ways forward: suggestions for a new comfort code

Driven by the imperatives of:

a) an increasingly rapidly warming world
b) flat-lining global economies, rising costs of fossil fuels, falling average incomes and growing levels of fuel poverty in many societies
c) the apparent inability of modern architects to change their modus operandi
d) a failing regulatory system that is not increasing building resilience to our changing climates

it is proposed here that Governments should require buildings to have:

1. **A thermal refuge plan** to include designated cool or warm rooms or areas in each building to which occupants can retreat during extreme heat and cold episodes, even when the power fails. A safe temperature band of between 10 °C and 35 °C (50 °F–95 °F) is recommended based on Nicol's research. Refuge spaces may include earth, sky and sun-coupled areas and ransom zones. In extreme outdoor climate, refuges can also be included.
2. **A natural energy mode** in which buildings can be occupied during power outages by opening windows for ventilation, and harvesting heat or coolth from managed natural heat and cold flows. Energy storage is also vital in extending the amount of time buildings can be run on natural energy and in the design and operation of thermal refuges in buildings.

When planning for an ideal low-carbon future all buildings should be able, for as much of any day or year as possible, to keep occupants comfortable by harvesting their energy needs from local natural sources of light, coolth and heat garnered from breezes and energy collected, stored and accessible when needed.

People will increasingly recognize the imperative for having everyday or occasional "thermal refuges" in their buildings as the climate warms increasingly rapidly. To ensure that these refuges are in the coldest or the warmest part of the building, people will have to learn about the fundamental heat flows through their spaces and structures.

The two innovative steps outlined in this chapter are:

a) Taking on board the proposed broader safe and acceptable occupied temperature limits above [10 °C–35 °C (50 °F–95 °F)] indoors in design guidance and regulations.
b) Factoring into design and facilitating the routine and occasional movements of people seeking warmth or coolth around thermally landscaped buildings.

These two steps would enable a far wider range of both indoor, and significantly, outdoor temperatures to be deemed and proven to be acceptable in well-designed buildings with thermal refuges, saving lives and impacting on economies. They would redirect us back to a new/old understanding of "active passive design." The lessons taught by Hay in his ingenious solar building systems and other creative activists of his time can provide the bedrock for an age of genuinely low-carbon buildings, keeping people safe when the power is on or off. Integrating heat and people flows through buildings will help us to "bounce forward" to safer, more resilient thermal landscapes in our buildings and cities.

Notes

1 Susan Roaf, Manuel Fuentes and Stephanie Thomas, *Ecohouse* (London: Routledge, 2014).
2 James Marston Fitch, *American Building: The Forces that Shaped It* (Cambridge, MA: The Riverside Press, 1966).
3 Fergus Nicol and Susan Roaf, "Rethinking Thermal Comfort," *Building Research Information* 45, no. 7 (March 2017): 711–716.
4 Boris Kingma, Arjan Frijns and Wouter Marken Lichtenbelt, "The Thermoneutral Zone: Implications for Metabolic Studies," *Frontiers in Bioscience* (Elite Edition), no. 4 (January 2012): 1975–1985, and Boris Kingma, Marcel Schweiker, Andreas Wagner and Wouter van Marken Lichtenbelt, "Exploring Internal Body Heat Balance to Understand Thermal Sensation," *Building Research & Information* 45, no. 7 (April 2017): 808–818.
5 Fergus Nicol, Michael Humphreys and Susan Roaf, *Adaptive Thermal Comfort: Principals and Practice* (London: Routledge, 2012).
6 Ackermann, Ibid., 80.
7 "Ensure operable windows," Urban Green Council, accessed July 2017, https://urbangreencouncil.org/sites/default/files/brtf_26-_ensure_operable_windows.pdf.
8 "Opinion," Stanford Law School, accessed July 2017, http://scocal.stanford.edu/opinion/beacon-residential-etc-assn-v-skidmore-owings-merrill-34333.
9 "A Pioneer Refuses to Fade Away: His Passion for Solar Still Burns," by Elizabeth Douglass *in LA Times*, accessed July 2017, http://articles.latimes.com/2007/nov/10/business/fi-haroldhay10.
10 E.E. Alders, "Adaptive Heating, Ventilation and Solar Shading for Dwellings," *Architectural Science Review* 60, no. 3, Special Issue (2017): 150–166.

14 Resilience as a driver of passive design

Alex Wilson

Harold Hay, Peter Van Dresser, Douglas Balcomb and other pioneers of passive solar design from the 1960s and '70s brilliantly laid the groundwork for the state-of-the-art building designs that can wean us from fossil fuels and help mitigate climate change in the decades ahead. They designed buildings that could operate passively through careful sizing and orientation of window apertures, smart building geometry, incorporation of thermal mass and strategic use of insulation. These buildings could capture a vast majority of their needed working energy from sunlight, store heat for nighttime use and prevent overheating during the summer months. Operating costs and environmental impacts of such buildings could be greatly reduced by avoiding fossil fuel and electricity use for space conditioning.

The potential of operating our buildings without fossil fuels was appealing to the burgeoning environmental movement. Passive solar design became a rallying cry for a generation of environmentalists who grew up being horrified by the Santa Barbara Oil Spill, Ohio's Cuyahoga River catching on fire and the haze of ozone smog that blanketed our urban skylines.

Despite excitement within the environmental community, passive solar design has not entered the mainstream of building design in North America. In part, this may be because passive solar design relies on commodity components – windows for solar heat gain and masonry components for heat storage, for example – rather than proprietary components that could realize monetary gains for manufacturers. But a more likely reason for the failure of passive solar design to go mainstream is that the motivation has been largely altruistic – doing the right thing. A more direct motivation is needed.

This chapter makes the case that an interest in keeping people safe and protecting them from the impacts of climate change can be a greater motivation for designing and building the type of systems that Hay and his fellow visionaries invented.

The emerging design criterion of passive survivability

When Hurricane Katrina struck New Orleans and the Gulf Coast on August 29, 2005, much of America watched helplessly on television as the tragedy unfolded. A group of architects associated with several Midwestern chapters of the U.S. Green Building Council and the Vermont company BuildingGreen, Inc. set out to do something about it. Within days of the hurricane making landfall, this team began planning a series of charrettes to be held in Atlanta during that fall. Green building experts from around the country worked with residents of the Gulf Coast to develop strategies for rebuilding in a more sustainable and resilient manner. Out of that initiative, *The New Orleans Principles* was published in late 2005.

One of the ten New Orleans Principles was to "Provide for passive survivability." As described in the document, "Homes, schools, public buildings, and neighborhoods should be designed and built or rebuilt to serve as livable refuges in the event of crisis or breakdown of energy, water, and sewer systems."[1] This principle emerged from the observation of how poorly many buildings in New Orleans performed when they lost power. New Orleans residents were evacuated to the Superdome, but because without power temperatures this space rose to 105 °F, it had to be subsequently evacuated. The stadium was not designed to function without electricity.

At the same time, charrette members observed that, without power, older homes often did better than new houses. In the Gulf Coast, many dwellings had been designed prior to the advent of air conditioning using principles of bioclimatic design or vernacular architecture: designs that work with local climates. These older homes incorporated architectural elements such as wrap-around porches that shaded windows from direct sun and designs that facilitated natural ventilation – channeling cool summer breezes through the buildings.

Participants in the 2005 Atlanta charrettes recognized that Hurricane Katrina would not be the last storm to cause an extended power outage in the region. Consequently, they argued to combine the wisdom of vernacular architecture with today's best materials. Houses and apartment buildings could be designed to maintain reasonably habitable conditions during power outages or interruptions in heating fuel.

BuildingGreen ran a series of articles promoting the concept of passive survivability and, in early 2012, spun off a nonprofit organization, the Resilient Design Institute (RDI), to advance our understanding of resilience and further its implementation. As defined by RDI, resilience is "the capacity to adapt to changing conditions and to maintain or regain functionality and vitality in the face of stress or disturbance. It is the capacity to bounce back after a disturbance or interruption."[2]

Why resilient design will become a growing motivation

The Intergovernmental Panel on Climate Change (IPCC) and other scientific bodies have been predicting that a warmer climate, and especially warmer water temperatures in the Gulf of Mexico and South Atlantic, will result in more intense storms. While individual storms, such as Hurricanes

Harvey, Irma and Maria in 2017, cannot be conclusively attributed to climate change, the "trend" of more intense storms like these can be attributed to climate change.[3]

Sea-level rise will exacerbate storm damage in coastal regions. Already by 2018, "sunny day or tidal flooding" has become a commonplace occurrence in places like Miami, Florida; Atlantic City, New Jersey; Annapolis, Maryland; Wilmington, North Carolina; and Charleston, South Carolina. When storm events coincide with high tides in these coastal areas, flooding can become severe. Along with inhibiting travel and daily business, such tidal flooding can affect power plants, which in coastal cities are typically built very close to sea level.

Winter storms, including extreme snowfall events, early snowstorms that strike before deciduous trees lose their leaves and ice storms, can bring down power lines, causing extensive outages. The February 2010 "Snowmageddon" storm wreaked havoc in the Mid-Atlantic region, as did Boston's "Snowmageddon" in the winter of 2014–15, which saw a record snowfall of over 110 inches, including nearly 65 inches in February 2015. On October 29, 2011, the Halloween Weekend Snowstorm knocked out power to over 800,000 Connecticut Light & Power customers, the last of whom did not recover power until November 9.

Drought and heat waves, other likely impacts of climate change, can also cause power outages. Drought-related wildfires in Texas have knocked out power in recent years and, more significantly, prolonged drought could result in outages through lack of cooling water for power plants. The vast majority (roughly 89 percent) of U.S. power plants are thermo-electric plants that use a heat source (coal, natural gas or nuclear fission) to create high-pressure steam that drives a steam turbine; cooling water is required to condense that steam back into water.[4] When rivers, lakes or reservoirs serve as the cooling-water source, severe drought can threaten power output when water levels drop too low to use for cooling.

During heat waves, air-conditioning loads are high, and the power grid can become more taxed. With less safety margin (excess generation over demand) the grid becomes more vulnerable, and power outages are more likely.

Shifts in population since the mid-twentieth century exacerbate risks due to hurricanes and sea-level rise, since many of the quickly growing southeastern states are vulnerable to both hurricanes and sea-level rise. According to the National Oceanic and Atmospheric Administration (NOAA), in 2010, approximately 123 million people – 39 percent of the U.S. population – were living in counties directly on the coast.[5]

Elements of passive survivability

Strategies for achieving passive survivability will be familiar to anyone schooled in the specifics of passive solar design. Some of these key elements include the following.

Well-insulated building envelope

The first and most important element of passive survivability is a well-insulated building envelope. This will minimize the amount of heat needed in the winter months to maintain habitable conditions if power is lost, and it will help maintain reasonable summer temperatures if air conditioning is not functioning (or not included at all, as Hay argued). Elements of a well-insulated building envelope include above-ground walls, below-ground (foundation) walls, slab-on-grade or basement floor slab and the roof or ceiling, fenestration (windows or glazings), exterior doors and airtightness.

For all of these components of the building envelope, R-value recommendations vary by climate zone. For insulation values to contribute substantively to passive survivability, they must be considerably higher than recommendations found in most other guidance, including the International Energy Conservation Code (IECC).[6] Insulation levels and window U-factors recommended by BuildingGreen (Fig. 14.1) should be adequate for this purpose.

RECOMMENDATIONS BY DOE CLIMATE ZONES FOR NORTH AMERICA

Assembly Area	Hot (Zones 1–2)		Moderate (Zones 3–4)		Cold (Zones 5–6)		Coldest (Zones 7–8)	
	IECC	BG	IECC	BG	IECC	BG	IECC	BG
BUILDING ENVELOPE R-VALUES								
Slab	0	0	0 / 10	10	10	15	10	25
Basement wall	0	10	5/13 / 10/13	20	15/19	30	15/19	40
Floor above vented crawl space	13	15	19	25	30	40	38	50
Above-grade walls (wood-framed)	13	15	20 or 13+5	25	20 or 13+5 / 20+5 or 13+10	40	20+5 or 13+10	50
Ceiling – Flat	30	50	38	49	49	49	49	70
Ceiling – Cathedral		40		40		50		60
FENESTRATION								
Window U-factor – E, W, N	NR / 0.40	0.35	0.35	0.25	0.32	0.2	0.32	0.15
Windows U-factor – South		0.35		0.35		0.25		0.15
Window SHGC – E, W, N	0.25	<0.2	0.25	0.40	<0.33	NR	NR	NR
Window SHGC – South	<0.3	>0.3		<0.4	>0.3	>0.5		>0.4
Exterior door (unit U-factor)	NA	0.3	NA	0.3	NA	0.25	NA	0.2
AIRTIGHTNESS								
Airtightness (ACH50)	NA	2	NA	2	NA	1.5	NA	1

Figure 14.1 BuildingGreen's R-value and U-factor recommendations for residential new construction.

Source: *The BuildingGreen Guide to Insulation*, Third Edition, 2017. Used by permission.

Notes on IECC requirements:

- Table references IECC 2012 code requirements.
- Divided columns indicate that requirements differ by the two climate zones shown, with the hotter climate zone appearing first.
- "15/19" means R-15 continuous insulation on the interior or exterior of the home or R-19 cavity insulation at the interior of the basement wall. "15/19" can be met with R-13 cavity insulation on the interior of the basement wall plus R-5 continuous insulation on the interior or exterior of the home.
- "13+5" means R-13 cavity insulation plus R-5 continuous insulation or insulated siding.
- While including prescriptive requirements such as installation of a continuous air barrier, IECC 2012 does not mandate a specific airtightness performance figure.
- NR: No recommendation.
- NA: Not applicable. IECC does not have specific requirements.

Notes on BuildingGreen recommendations:

- R-values are for whole-wall or true R-values in which thermal bridging through higher-conductivity materials has been taken into account.
- For R-values, recommendations are for equal or greater than listed values.
- For U-factors, recommendations are for equal or lower than listed values.
- For SHGC values, recommendations may be greater or lesser than listed values, so greater-than or less-than symbols are shown.
- Unvented crawlspaces should be insulated at the perimeter using basement wall recommendations.

Passive solar heating

In a long-term power outage without a back-up heating system, indoor temperatures in even the most heavily insulated building will approach outside ambient levels in winter if there is not a heating source; in many regions, passive solar can provide that heat source. In the 1960s and '70s, passive solar pioneers like Hay taught us how to use building design to capture heat from the sun through windows, roofs and other glazing areas during the winter months. They taught us also how to store heat in thermal mass on a daily basis, and to distribute it to provide some or all of a building's heating requirements.

While the passive solar pioneers taught us the principles of passive solar design as a way to save energy and money, those design features become even more important following natural disasters when electricity may not be available or in the event of interruption of heating fuel supplies. In these situations, rather than simply saving energy, passive solar design can keep people alive in their shelters.

The difference with state-of-the-art passive solar design today, compared with passive solar during Hay's time, is that building components, especially glazings, have improved dramatically. We can now tune glazings through orientation by specifying different types of low-emissivity coatings – altering both the amount of sunlight transmitted and the amount of heat loss – and in this way allow ore uniform placement of glazing apertures even while producing significantly different solar gain performance.

Cooling load avoidance

A key aspect of passive survivability is to keep unwanted solar gain out of a building during warmer months so that the building will remain habitable if it loses power. This involves the same principles advanced by Hay and others: building orientation, geometry and shading features to take advantage of the varying sun path across the sky throughout the year. In addition, limiting the glass area or using low-solar-heat-gain glazings on the east and west facades of a building constitute some of the basic principles to avoid cooling load. Operable shading devices can be particularly important as emergency cooling-load-avoidance measures, since they can be operated manually as needed.

Natural ventilation

An important passive survivability strategy is to provide natural ventilation that takes advantage of prevailing summer breezes and the buoyancy of warmer air rising in a building. Some natural ventilation strategies use earth tubes to pre-cool the incoming fresh air, though care must be taken to ensure that such earth tubes do not grow mold and introduce mold spores to the building. During Hurricane Katrina in 2005, we saw the risks of not providing natural ventilation. In several hospitals where patients could not be evacuated, the lack of operable windows caused temperatures in their rooms to rise above 100 °F, contributing to numerous fatalities. In some situations, nursing staff used chairs to break windows and provide ventilation.

The risks posed by a lack of natural ventilation were taken to heart by the designers of Spaulding Rehabilitation Hospital in the Charlestown section of Boston, for which design was just beginning when Hurricane Katrina struck New Orleans. Spaulding became the first modern hospital in the U.S. to incorporate operable windows in all patient rooms when it was completed in 2013. The hospital included other passive survivability features including triple glazing on all windows, higher-than-normal insulation levels and exterior shading systems to control solar heat gain.[7]

High humidity in the eastern United States can make natural ventilation more difficult than in Europe, but during times of emergency, when the power grid is down, accepting higher humidity levels than are typically considered comfortable is reasonable. Thus, it may make sense to design "dual-mode" edifices: buildings that normally rely on conventional, mechanical systems to maintain comfortable temperature and humidity (without natural ventilation), but that can also be operated in an emergency mode with natural ventilation, helping to keep people safe during extended power outages.

Passive cooling

Solar chimneys draw air into a building through buried earth tubes and wind catchers transmit coolth through their tower mass cooled at night through night-sky radiation. Both can passively cool a space to below the ambient outdoor temperature and both of these systems are primarily designed to enhance natural ventilation. The Skytherm system, designed in the 1960s by Hay and described elsewhere in this book, is uniquely designed for dependable passive cooling and heating. In a situation in which power is lost in a hot, dry climate, this passive cooling technology can deliver highly effective cooling and help to achieve passive survivability.

Consistent passive cooling is very difficult to achieve. For various reasons, Hay's Skytherm system has never gained market penetration beyond a few prototype projects, but growing awareness in resilience and, specifically, passive survivability could revive interest in such an ingenious system.

Photovoltaics and electricity storage

The final element of passive survivability stretches the normal definition of "passive": a photovoltaic (PV) array that generates electricity from sunlight, and a battery storage system to store that electricity for times when the grid is not functioning. Such a PV system can still be grid-tied (as are the vast majority of PV systems in the U.S. today), but it is designed so that it can operate in an islanding mode when the grid is down and the system is safely disconnected from the grid. Some inverters – devices that convers a PV array's direct-current (DC) output into alternating current (AC) – can operate in both grid-tied and islanding mode. Some other systems require a different inverter (or inverters) for operation in an islanding mode.

The future may see the development of more sophisticated variations on this theme – such as plug-in electric vehicles that provide the back-up battery storage. With this approach, rather than the battery system sitting idly the vast majority of the time and used only during power outages, the batteries would be used all the time by the vehicle. Utility companies may eventually rely on such vehicles to help them manage peak electricity loads through controls that allow a plugged-in vehicle to send power back into the grid when the power is most needed.

Quantifying passive survivability

As the country (and world) experiences more frequent storms and other disturbances that cause power outages, there is likely to be a demand for metrics of passive survivability and a methodology for predicting whether a building will, indeed, maintain habitable temperatures should it lose power for an extended period of time. The Resilient Design Institute and the Resilience Working Group of the U.S. Green Building Council have been working on definitions and metrics of passive survivability – or "thermal habitability" – since 2012.

With this effort, the first task was to define what constitutes "habitable conditions." It is not only about air temperature; humidity also plays an important role. Consider two buildings that lose power during the summer months: one in Phoenix and another in Miami. If the indoor temperature rises to 90 °F in both buildings, the Phoenix building will be far more habitable, because the low relative humidity means that moisture can readily evaporate from an occupant's skin, causing evaporative cooling. Using the metric of standard effective temperature (SET) rather than air temperature as the metric for passive survivability is one way to factor in humidity. Another potential metric is wet bulb globe temperature (WBGT).

RDI and the USGBC Resilience Working Group arrived at a "habitability zone" of 54 °F to 86 °F SET (12 °C to 30 °C SET). While more physiology studies will be needed to determine if this is the right temperature range, it is at least a starting point. For people of average health, maintaining temperature and humidity conditions within this range will avoid the most extreme reactions: hypothermia, hyperthermia and death. With adequate blankets or outdoor clothing in the winter months, and some air flow in the summer months, most people will likely be safe within this temperature range.

Once an acceptable temperature/humidity range is identified, thermal modeling of a building can be used to determine whether those conditions will be maintained in the building. The thermal modeling software has to be able to represent the thermal performance with mechanical equipment off, but most of the leading products are able to do this.

Final thoughts

The pioneers of passive solar design did the hard work of figuring out how to heat and cool buildings passively. Many solar energy activists believed that those features would quickly be adopted in building design. They were not. Heating and cooling our buildings with fossil fuels and electricity became simply too easy and, for most Americans, reasonably affordable.

Designing and building our homes, apartment buildings, schools and other critical-use buildings today to rely on passive design is fairly hard: we have to use better insulation and more expensive windows, we have to place windows in the right places, orient the building properly, incorporate thermal mass in the right places and provide for ventilation – it all takes effort. With conventional fuel-fired or electric HVAC equipment, we simply have to tell the mechanical contractor how much heating and cooling is needed and where to place the equipment.

With the growing number of tragedies triggered by climate change, resilient design is increasingly important. The growing desire to create buildings that will keep occupants safe if they lose power calls for a renewed look at passive design. The solutions would be familiar to Hay and his fellow pioneers from forty-plus years ago, but the motivation is different. These buildings will keep us safer in an age of more intense storms, sea-level rise, wildfires and even terrorism. We can incorporate requirements for passive survivability into building codes as life-safety regulations.

Adoption of passive survivability as an element of resilient design will not only help to keep us safe in our homes, apartments and schools, but it will help to mitigate the global climate change that is exacerbating many of these risks. By looking back into what Hay and his peers invented decades ago, we can glimpse key principles of a resilient design future.

Notes

1 *The New Orleans Principles* (U.S. Green Building Council, 2005), 19.
2 Resilient Design Institute, "What is Resilience?," accessed December 21, 2017, www.resilientdesign.org/what-is-resilience.
3 Committee on Extreme Weather Events and Climate Change Attribution, *Attribution of Extreme Weather Events in the Context of Climate Change* (Washington, DC: National Academy of Sciences, 2016).
4 Paul A. Torcellini, N. Long and Ron Judkoff, *Consumptive Water Use for U.S. Power Production* (Golden, CO: National Renewable Energy Laboratory, 2003).
5 National Ocean Service (NOAA), Washington, DC, "What Percentage of the American Population Lives Near the Coast?," accessed December 21, 2017, https://oceanservice.noaa.gov/facts/population.html.
6 International Code Council, *2018 International Energy Conservation Code* (Country Club Hills, IL: International Code Council, Inc., 2017).
7 Alex Wilson, "How to Make a Hospital Resilient: A Tour of Spaulding Rehab," *Resilient Design Institute Website* (February 2015), accessed December 21, 2017, www.resilientdesign.org/how-to-make-a-hospital-resilient-a-tour-of-spaulding-rehabilitation-center.

15 From survivability to thrivability

Finding joy in passive design

Vikram Sami

Central air conditioning has become ubiquitous in the United States. Relatively cheap power, increased expectations for thermal comfort, and rising temperatures – especially in urban areas – have all contributed to the pervasiveness of and dependency on A/C systems. A recent article in *The New York Times* entitled "How Air-Conditioning Conquered America (Even the Pacific Northwest)" looks at housing trends in the U.S. from the 1940s to the present. The authors found that only 33 percent of homes built before the 1940s have central air conditioning, while in recent construction that proportion goes up to 88 percent.[1]

Anecdotally, practicing architecture in Seattle – home to one of the mildest climates in the United States – I have witnessed this market shift firsthand. It can be a challenge to even convince developers to incorporate operable windows into their office building projects. As HVAC (heating, ventilation and air conditioning) systems become more efficient and renewable energy gets cheaper, there is not much of an energy penalty for leaving them out.

Within such a context, what is the role of passive design in architecture? Everything seems to be stacked against its success in today's world in terms of cost, efficiency, and convenience. Is there any room left for creative design proposals that rise above commodity and resist valuation solely in terms of cost. How can architecture prioritize connectivity among communities, as well as healthier, resilient environments? Could designing passive buildings make for thoughtful, interesting architecture; resilient, connected communities; and healthier, more mindful occupants?

Although passive solar design gained popularity in the mid-20th century, its roots reach back much farther. Until the advent of modern air conditioning, passive design strategies were the only way to attain thermal comfort, especially in challenging climates. As a result, passive design that worked with the climate became an integral part of architecture, sometimes inspiring particular ritualistic or social behavior. A good example of this can be seen in the Anasazi cliff dwellings in the Southwest United States, a region that becomes very hot in the daytime during summer, but cools rapidly at night. Inversely, during winter it becomes very cold, but with abundant sunlight. Built into the south face of a cliff, partially nestled under an outcropping, the dwellings take advantage of all the climatic variations in this region. The Mesa Verde cliff dwelling is another demonstration of diurnal and seasonal passive adaptation. In the summer, the heavy mass of the adobe and rock cools off at night, providing a daytime refuge in the shade of the cliff's natural overhang. During winter, the settlement is bathed in sunlight from the lower winter sun. The dwelling's thermal mass stores heat for the cold winter nights. The settlement's passive design implementation is also manifest in the Anasazi's social patterns: they would migrate between the indoors and outdoors seasonally and diurnally, retreating to the indoors in the daytime in summer, and nighttime in the winter.[2]

There are numerous historic examples of passive systems developed around the world, each unique to its climate. What is common to these systems is that they all manifest overt expressions of their thermal function – whether it is in the delightfully intricate *jaali* walls in India that provide shade and ventilation or the Mughal gardens where water becomes a visual element but also provides passive cooling to the occupants, or even simple porches, courtyards, and swings. These passive systems create sensory experiences that amplify one's appreciation of their surroundings.

Passive systems also serve an important social function. In New York City, as well as in many other places, before air conditioning, it was common for people to sit out on the streets or on stoops during hot days because it was too hot inside. As a result, neighbors knew one another well and watched over the streets. With the advent of air conditioning, we have become a more insular society, preferring to keep to ourselves indoors, ceding our sense of shared ownership of the streets along with our use of public space as a backdrop for building relationships.

Thermal variance created by passive systems is seen as a negative because of certain drawbacks, especially in speculative buildings. Purely active systems are used to prevent complaints that spaces are too hot or too cold. A 2009 survey conducted by IFMA found that air temperature complaints far outweighed any other complaints that tenants voiced about their spaces, and that most complaints in offices were reporting over-conditioning rather than under-conditioning.[3] In a 2015 blog post, Lindsay Baker, president of Comfy (an application that controls space temperature), studied responses from users at temperatures from 66 °F–78 °F; she found that there was not universal agreement on comfort on any point[4] (Fig. 15.1). Clearly, humans are built for thermal variance. Furthermore, thermal variance gives people a reason to gather: primitive humans around a fire, urban kids on a stoop, or elderly folks on a porch. In her book *Thermal Delight in Architecture*, Lisa Heschong gives an account of an American family moving to a French village. The family found that during the winter, the fireplace became the focal point of their family life, while in the summer, their social life became more public, moving out into the streets and marketplaces.[5] Thermal variation was the original social network – bringing people together.

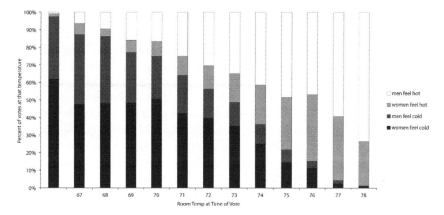

Figure 15.1 Thermal comfort graph showing responses at different temperatures.
Source: © Lindsay Baker.

However, two of the main roadblocks to the widespread adoption of passive design are the convenience of active systems and the current state of technology. The instant gratification and expediency of controlling air temperature at the flick of a switch is a luxury that fits contemporary lifestyles. Since the invention of air-conditioning systems in the early 20th century, modern consumers have come to expect the instant change of environments generated by automated devices that require minimal human involvement. However, this instantaneity has generated long-term environmental consequences.

From an architect's point of view, it would be easier not to have to think about thermal comfort issues. The convenience of having mechanical engineers tackle the field of thermal comfort with horsepower has become second nature to many practitioners. Thermal comfort has become one of the biggest selling points of centralized air conditioning. However, it is important to remember that thermal comfort is not a guarantee when using an HVAC system. While air conditioning promises the ability to control an environment's temperature, with the intent of achieving thermal comfort, the latter is rarely achieved solely by mechanical means.

Thermal comfort is widely acknowledged to be based on six factors: air temperature, mean radiant temperature, relative humidity, air movement, clothing levels, and metabolic rates.[6] However, most HVAC systems actually control only two aspects of thermal comfort: air temperature and relative humidity. Only really high-end HVAC systems address radiant temperatures. However, most thermostats only read air temperature, so in essence an HVAC system is being controlled by air temperature, even if it is a radiant system. The use of active conditioning systems is driven by a heightened desire for convenience. An unfortunate byproduct is that occupants become detached from the operation of their buildings, as well as disengaged from their larger social and environmental context.

Inversely, well-designed passive systems can provide comfort through the careful manipulation of multiple factors. A passive solar house, for example, stores solar heat for use at night when temperatures drop. Heat distribution occurs through radiation and occupants can add to their personal insulation by putting on a sweater if the radiation alone is not warm enough for their comfort. In the summer, occupants control radiation by using exterior shading devices. They can open windows to increase airflow, particularly at night to precool the mass and provide radiative cooling in the daytime.

It is then somewhat of a paradox that active systems promote passive users, and passive systems tend to produce active occupants who are in tune with their building, context, and climate. Passive systems are more than just buildings – they are a confluence of people, place, and program, relying on users who are in tune with their surroundings, and their building.

Thermal comfort is a complex issue, and difficult to predict using analytical tools. When architects incorporate passive systems into their projects, they tend to use vague rules of thumb that do not give designers flexibility to test new ideas. As a result, we tend to keep relying on engineers to tell us when building envelopes hinder system performance and leave it at that.

Some popular energy modeling programs today, such as eQUEST or TRACE, accurately predict energy use from lights, plug loads, and HVAC systems, but are not as effective in predicting thermal comfort factors other than air temperature. Furthermore, most of these programs use "lumped node" models to calculate space temperatures, wherein a thermal zone is simplified to have a single temperature at any point in time.[7] Doing this saves computing time and allows for manageable simulation times. However, the results are based on a hermetically sealed, mechanically controlled space with very little external stimuli. When designing passive systems, these programs fall short in capturing the subtle variations within a space, which are crucial in making a passive system work. Some of the popular energy modeling tools in use today cannot even calculate mean radiant temperatures within a space and cannot simulate natural ventilation airflow, either wind- or buoyancy-driven.

Newer simulation tools at an architect's disposal, such as IESVE, are capable of predicting subtle variations in thermal conditions across a space, mean radiant temperatures, ventilation through operable windows, stack ventilation, and a variety of other factors. Where architects have abdicated creative responsibility of the thermal building performance to engineers, we now have the opportunity to reclaim and test out design ideas iteratively. This should allow architects to bring new thinking into the field of passive design, moving past rules of thumb and checklists.

One of the reasons passive systems have found their way back (albeit in a very small measure) into the profession is due to the notion of resilience and the ability to adapt to and bounce back from potentially catastrophic events. In recent times, we have witnessed an increasing number of catastrophic climate events, especially in the Southeast United States. Communities hit by hurricanes in this region have had their utility grids cut off and were forced to make do without electricity for days, sometimes weeks, which can render buildings uninhabitable and even dangerous. In the aftermath of Hurricane Irma in 2017, twelve people died in a Miami nursing home from overheating after the building lost power and air conditioning. Similarly, patients were evacuated from New York hospitals after Hurricane Sandy knocked out power to those facilities in 2012. Healthcare facilities are arguably the most at risk, but this is an issue that affects all buildings. This is not only true for coastal locations – some areas of Atlanta faced more than forty-eight hours without power after Hurricane Irma – or limited to weather events. In 2003, the Northeast United States and parts of Canada experienced a grid outage that left 50 million people without power for two days. With the growing popularity of centrally air-conditioned buildings, we are also increasingly more reliant on the stability of our electric grid to make our buildings habitable. The result is a current building stock that is progressively unusable during times of power outages, which is why the notion of resiliency has become more important in design.

In 2005 after Hurricane Katrina, Alex Wilson of BuildingGreen coined the term "passive survivability" (covered in Chapter 14); that is, the ability of a building to maintain critical life support systems in the event of a loss of power.[8] While valid and much needed, this way of thinking only addresses an alternative response to critical situations. To overcome this, it seems that we need to reflect upon the possibility of integrating passive energy thinking in our contemporary everyday life. Therefore, I propose an additional consideration that builds upon Wilson's thought, one that I call "passive thrivability."

Passive thrivability is a mindset shift whereby we are not simply looking at passive systems as something we use to wait out the storm – an emergency system to be called upon once every three to four years when the power goes out – but rather a way to improve and influence the quality of everyday life. What if we explore the nuances of thermal aesthetics as proposed by Lisa Heschong: designing experiences that heighten our perception and appreciation of our thermal environment instead of deadening it? Focusing only on emergencies devalues the potential of passive systems, resulting in under-designed afterthoughts. Instead, what if we design passive systems that can work with and for everyday usage? Such arrangements would be easy to operate, they would provoke users' engagement, and they could improve people's overall experience of a building.

In practice, the notion of passive thrivability results in different designs for every project. The better the system, the more it is customized to the user, the climate, and the particular building type, successfully bringing together people, place, and program. As an example, architect Tom Kundig of Olson Kundig designed the Wagner Education Center at the Center for Wooden Boats (CWB) in Seattle, Washington, a non-profit organization that, amongst other things, teaches the community about wooden boat heritage and sailing. Designed for passive cooling in the relatively mild summer months – the building has no air conditioning – the occupants will interact with it as they would with a boat. The implementation of passive energy design for this project, which opens to the public in the fall of 2018, mirrors the central tenet of sailing: that one must work with the natural forces to make adjustments to optimize performance (Fig. 15.2).

SUMMER DAY - NATURAL VENTILATION

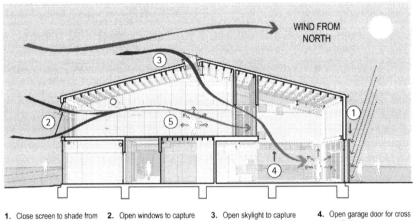

1. Close screen to shade from summer sun
2. Open windows to capture prevailing northerly winds
3. Open skylight to capture prevailing northerly winds
4. Open garage door for cross ventilation
5. Radiant exchange with cool surfaces

SUMMER NIGHT - NIGHT FLUSH COOLING

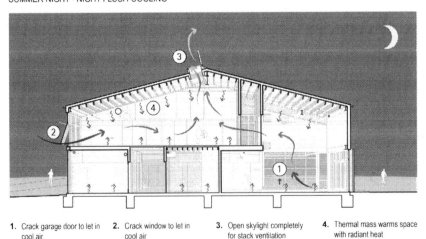

1. Crack garage door to let in cool air
2. Crack window to let in cool air
3. Open skylight completely for stack ventilation
4. Thermal mass warms space with radiant heat

Figure 15.2 Center for Wooden Boats Wagner Education Center, Seattle, WA.
Source: © Olson Kundig.

CWB is oriented along an east–west axis to minimize the low sun angles from the east and west facades, and to maximize winter sun in the building, which is scarce in Seattle. There is also a movable exterior shade system on the south designed to minimize solar heat gain in the summer. The building's large operable doors and windows, as well as a series of operable skylights, are designed to naturally ventilate the building, which is done by hand rather than automated and controlled by a computerized system. Whereas modern passive buildings of this type tend to use elaborate temperature sensor networks, computerized data management, and mechanical actuators to optimize the performance of the system, in this building, the users are the system, acting as sensors, actuators, and data storage. To achieve optimal comfort, occupants must be educated about how to use and adapt to their building.

At CWB, the design of the passive system does not stop with the building. Olson Kundig's design team is currently working with stakeholders to develop best practices to tune comfort, from opening windows at night to precool the building for the next day, to determining the best time of day to deploy the shades. The project will be a learning experience for both designer and client, and the hope is that the building will improve in performance as the users learn about their building. Because the project has a large public component with the classrooms, it will also be an investigation into community decision-making relative to passive performance – connecting visitors who might be there for only a few classes with regular occupants in how they run the space and its impact on their comfort. The success of the building depends on sustained user engagement, which in return creates a sense of physical and emotional appropriation.

Thermal comfort, by definition, is the lack of discomfort. However, the way we approach our thermal environments is not with a mindset to provide pleasure – it is more about reducing displeasure. The distinction, while subtle, is important. It means, in essence, that we create thermal environments that are meant to reduce awareness of our surroundings. The hermetically sealed boxes designed to keep the climate out are often sensory deprivation chambers.

Passive design inherently promotes mindfulness of place and time. It celebrates its connection to climate through the actions of users. It is a lifestyle shift, sometimes requiring occupants to think beyond the immediacy of their situation. The way a building performs at night might affect users' thermal comfort during the daytime, and vice versa.

Apart from an increase in mindfulness and a greater awareness of one's surroundings, there may be physiological benefits in embracing passive systems and natural variations in temperature. In a 2012 article published through the National Institute of Health's National Library of Medicine titled, "Ambient Temperature and Obesity," authors Douglas Moellering and Daniel Smith suggest there may be correlations between obesity rates and the prevalence of climate control.[9] To offset this, the authors recommend exposure to natural variations in our thermal conditions.

The concept of passive thrivability is rooted in the belief that buildings that engage with their environment are inherently more joyful. Good passive design always embraces climate – it looks for opportunities in environmental conditions and program wherever possible and shelters from the climate when needed. By celebrating the connection to nature, buildings designed for passive energy performance go beyond framing views through a window and expose a variety of local environmental qualities. The building becomes one *with* the place instead of one *in* it.

Architect Tom Kundig describes this distinction when he talks about how growing up in a mid-century modern home was a source of frustration for him. "Transparency," he says, "was always a promise, not a reality."[10] Glass was a lie, a partition that separated the indoors from the outdoors. "You were either in an aquarium or looking into one."[11] Kundig's buildings are designed to forge a direct connection to nature, often using simple machines to dissolve the boundaries between inside and outside. "These projects are trying to embrace the natural existing condition as much as possible," he says.[12]

Olson Kundig's office is located on the top two-and-a-half floors of an old shoe factory building in the historic Pioneer Square neighborhood of Seattle. At the center of the space, a large skylight designed by Tom Kundig in collaboration with kinetic engineer, Phil Turner, is operated by an elegant hydraulic system that runs off the city water mains. When the 15-foot-wide skylight opens, it shuts down the HVAC system, and an email goes out telling people they can open their windows. The historic building is poorly insulated and leaky as a sieve. Allowing it to perform on a passive system such as this makes it infinitely more efficient. However, the real attraction of the skylight goes beyond BTUs (Fig. 15.3).

The first thing one notices when the skylight opens is an awakening of the senses. The white noise from the HVAC system disappears. The ambient sounds coming from outside the building, like those of birds and street noises, mingle with the acoustic reality of the office. Suddenly, one becomes aware of subtle breezes and thermal variations in different parts of the building. The direct daylight begins to affect the materials and, consequently, people's perception of them. The skylight is one of the first stops on any tour of our office. It is heartening to see an office of 170 occupants take such pride in what is essentially a passive design feature.

What makes the skylight special is that, rather than being automated, it is a manually operated system. While automated operation could save a little energy and help optimize the system, the manual user engagement provides a more pleasurable physical experience. Every time the skylight is opened or shut, it is a conscious decision made by one or two people and shared with the rest of the office. It is an event within the daily life of the workers,

Figure 15.3 Skylight, Olson Kundig office, Seattle, WA.
Source: Photograph © Benjamin Benschneider.

a testament to the fact that passive design is still alive, and that it can be joyous, thoughtful, and mindfully designed.

Notes

1 Emily Badger and Alan Blinder, "How Air-Conditioning Conquered America (Even the Pacific Northwest)," *The New York Times* (August 4, 2017), accessed

December 11, 2017, www.nytimes.com/2017/08/04/upshot/the-all-conquering-air-conditioner.html?_r=0.

2   Jason F. McLennan, *The Philosophy of Sustainable Design: The Future of Architecture* (Kansas City, MO: Ecotone Publishing, 2004), 16.

3   "Temperature Wars: Savings vs. Comfort," *International Facility Management Association Survey* (2009), accessed December 11, 2017, www.ifma.org/docs/default-source/surveys/hvacsurvey2009.pdf?sfvrsn=2.

4   Lindsay Baker, "Women Chilly At Work? Yes, But … It's Complicated," *Comfy Blog* (August 5, 2015), accessed December 11, 2017, www.comfyapp.com/blog/women-chilly-at-work-yes-but-its-complicated.

5   Lisa Heschong, *Thermal Delight in Architecture* (Boston, MA: MIT Press, 1979).

6   P.O. Fanger, *Thermal Comfort* (New York: McGraw-Hill, 1973) and ANSI/ASHRAE Standard 55, "Thermal Environmental Conditions for Human Occupancy," 2017, accessed December 11, 2017, www.techstreet.com/ashrae/standards/ashrae-55 2017?product_id=1994974&ashrae_auth_token.

7   For further discussion of the conventional "lumped node" approach, see Vikram Sami and Joshua Gassman, "A Simultaneous Modelling Methodology to Analyze Passive Solar Performance of Trombe Walls," paper presented at PLEA2006, September 6–8, 2006, and Vikram Sami, "Applying Computational Fluid Dynamics to Analyze Natural Ventilation and Human Comfort in Buildings," *SOLAR 2003: Proceedings of the Annual Conference of the American Solar Energy Society* (Austin, TX: American Solar Energy Society, 2003): 851–856.

8   Alex Wilson, "Green Building: Passive Survivability and Building Codes," *Building Safety Journal* 6 (October–November 2008).

9   Douglas R. Moellering and Daniel L. Smith, Jr., "Ambient Temperature and Obesity," *Current Obesity Reports, PMC*, 1, no. 1 (March 2012): 26–34.

10 Tom Kundig as quoted in Liz Stinson, "Tom Kundig's Buildings Are Half Machine, Half Architecture," *WIRED* (November 23, 2015), accessed December 11, 2017, www.wired.com/2015/11/tom-kundigs-buildings-are-half-machine-half-architecture.

11 Ibid.

12 Ibid.

Index